COMMUNICATION AND INFORMATION TECHNOLOGY

MES-32

Notes For

Master of Arts (Education) (MAEDU)

Useful For

IGNOU, KSOU (Karnataka), Bihar University (Muzaffarpur), Nalanda University, Jamia Millia Islamia, Vardhman Mahaveer Open University (Kota), Uttarakhand Open University, Kurukshetra University, Seva Sadan's College of Education (Maharashtra), Lalit Narayan Mithila University, Andhra University, Pt. Sunderlal Sharma (Open) University (Bilaspur), Annamalai University, Bangalore University, Bharathiar University, Bharathidasan University, HP University, Centre for distance and open learning, Kakatiya University (Andhra Pradesh), KOU (Rajasthan), MPBOU (MP), MDU (Haryana), Punjab University, Tamilnadu Open University, Sri Padmavati Mahila Visvavidyalayam (Andhra Pradesh), Sri Venkateswara University (Andhra Pradesh), UCSDE (Kerala), University of Jammu, YCMOU, Rajasthan University, UPRTOU, Kalyani University, Banaras Hindu University (BHU) and all other Indian Universities.

GullyBaba Publishing House Pvt. Ltd.

ISO 9001 & ISO 14001 CERTIFIED CO.

Regd. Office:
2525/193, 1st Floor, Onkar Nagar-A,
Tri Nagar, Delhi-110035
(From Kanhaiya Nagar Metro Station Towards Old Bus Stand)
Call: 9991112299, 9312235086
WhatsApp: 9350849407

Branch Office:
1A/2A, 20, Hari Sadan,
Ansari Road, Daryaganj,
New Delhi-110002
Ph.011-45794768
Call & WhatsApp:
8130521616,8130511234

E-mail: hello@gullybaba.com, **Website**: GullyBaba.com

New Edition

Author: Gullybaba.com Panel

Disclaimer

Although the author and publisher have made every effort to ensure that the information in this notes is correct, the author and publisher do not assume and hereby disclaim any liability to any party for any loss, damage, or disruption caused by errors or omissions, whether such errors or omissions result from negligence, accident, or any other cause.

If you find any kind of error, please let us know and get reward and or the new notes free of cost.

The notes is based on IGNOU syllabus. This is only a sample. The notes/author/publisher does not impose any guarantee or claim for full marks or to be passed in exam. You are advised only to understand the contents with the help of this notes and answer in your words.

All disputes with respect to this publication shall be subject to the jurisdiction of the Courts, Tribunals and Forums of New Delhi, India only.

About Publisher

Gullybaba Publishing House is the brainchild of Mr Dinesh Verma, his name alone evokes profound respect and admiration. He is the pioneer of providing quality materials to the students of IGNOU because, having been a student of IGNOU, he understood the difficulty and pain of the non-availability of quality materials himself. He is serving the students with the following services:

EXAM-SUCCESS GUIDES

Important questions, solved question papers, guess papers - all in one! to score good marks in lesser time and effort.

FREE BOOK

As our love and care for our students, here is a Free Gift – A Famous Book "Secrets to Pass IGNOU Exams with Less Study" for you. You can download it now! https://www.gullybaba.com/ignou-free/

YOUR CONTRIBUTION TO MOTHER-EARTH

When you read our books, you save our mother earth as we use recycled paper to make these books. On every purchase, we contribute something to plant a plant.

SOLVED ASSIGNMENTS PDFs / HAND-WRITTEN

Best and genuine solved assignments PDFs you can instantly download from Gullybaba.com or our App.

PROJECT REPORTS/SYNOPSIS

Best Quality No-Rejection projects/synopsis by professionals researchers in ready to refer format.

MOBILE APP

You can download 'Gullybaba' app from Google Play Store to enjoy all above services at one place.

Notable Information

An attempt has been carefully made to present this book more useful and meet the requirement and challenges of the course prescribed by IGNOU University. We hope that this effort will fulfil the readers' expectations and help them excel in exams. Referring to University study material alongside this book is like "icing on the cake".

We wish you a successful and rewarding career. If you have any feedback to improve our books/products, please email at feedback@gullybaba.com. Because we believe, "Feedback is breakfast of champions" and our readers are our strength.

Table of Contents

Question Papers

Chapter-1

Communication Process

Q1. What do you mean by communication? Write the functions of communication.

Or

Discuss the concept of communication.

Or

What are the aspects of communication?

Ans. Communication is paramount in education. Whether it is teacher to student, student to student, teacher to teacher, teacher to parent, teacher to admin or admin to parent, or vice versa, communication is needed. It facilitates sharing of common experiences with others. It involves sharing of an idea, thought, feeling or information with others, which includes thinking, dreaming, speaking, arguing and so on. Thus, the scope of communication is very wide. Communication is part skill, part art and part science. It is a skill as it involves certain fundamental techniques, it is an art as it involves creative challenges, and it is science because certain verifiable principles are involved in making communication more effective.

Communication is the exchange and flow of information and ideas from one person to another; it involves a sender transmitting an idea, information, or feeling to a receiver. The word communication is derived from a Latin word "communis", which means 'to impart' or 'to make common'. It refers to a natural activity of all humans, which is to convey opinions, feelings, information, and ideas to other through words, body language or signs. George Vardhan defines effective communication as "purposive symbolic interchange resulting in workable understanding and agreement between the sender and the receiver". This interchange of information, ideas and thoughts may occur via different modes of communication like words (oral and written), signs and gestures.

Emphasising the processes of telling, listening, and understanding involved in the act of communicating with other people, Keith Davis says that communication is "the transfer of information and understanding from one person to another person. It is a way of reaching others with facts, ideas thoughts and values. It is a bridge of meaning among people so that they can share what they feel and know. By using this bridge, a person can cross safely the river of misunderstanding that sometimes separate people."

Functions of Communication: As we need communication to do, learn, understand and teach various things in the process of communication, thence communication have many functions which are as follows:

(1) Socialisation: It is the foremost function of Communication. As communication boost socialisation, so is socialisation do for communication. Communication fosters the feeling of oneness in a society by exposing the various social groups to different views. It develops the need to share and understand the feelings, emotios, hopes, aspirations and expectations of varied groups in a social system. Communication among teachers and learners makes socialisation possible in teaching-learning process.

(2) Motivation: Motivation is actively played a role to mobilise the society. Communication motivates and persuades individuals to meet the mutually agreed upon goals. Sharing success stories of those who have overcome the odds in life and have been able to achieve their goals can do this. This function of communication, although relevant in all walks of life is more pronounced in business and industry where communication is being increasingly used as a tool for motivation. When society is motivated, it turn learners attitude towards learning.

(3) Persuasion: Yet another important function of communication is to persuade. This may be to influence us towards a new idea, technique or a product and also to persuade us to buy these products. The industrial and corporate houses and advertising agencies, while taking messages of new products to potential consumers far and wide have amply exploited this function. Different mass communication media are used for this purpose. However, many a time unscrupulous advertisers tend to exploit the receiver of communication for ulterior motives. In the wake of globalisation and liberalisation and the growing competitive environment and consumerist culture, we need to take great care to understand the motives of the source.

(4) Sharing of Information: For good communication sharing of information is essential and here communication plays an important role in information dissemination related to any form of human activity, such as social, political, economic, educational and developmental. Regular exposure to information over a period of time generates awareness on a given issue, problem or matter of concern. To illustrate, if you were not informed about global warming or Pluto losing the status of a planet or the latest technology used in governance, your awareness on these issues would not have been there. So, communication provides us with information about the environment we are placed in. It helps in moulding our opinions, formulating decisions and in turn making 'informed choices' to safeguard our interests as well those of the society.

(5) Education and Training: Communication results in sharing of information, which in turn makes people knowledgeable and thus productive members of the society. Right from our childhood we are tought by our teachers in the school and elders at home and we thus gain various new concepts and skills as we grow up. However, we do not cease to learn when we grow up as we continue to learn throughout our lives. In the modern educational scenario, training of personnel is an ongoing process and communication plays an important role in orientation and training of teachers and learners. The degree of learning depends to a great extent not only on the content of training but also how effectively the information and skills are shared. As we know, knowledge can be constructed through interaction between learners and his/her peers and also with his/her teachers/sources of information. Hence, effective communication results in effective teaching and training.

(6) Preservation of culture: Communication helps to preserve the culture and heritage of a nation and society. Through communication, stories from the epics, such as Ramayana, Mahabharata, Bible, Koran, etc. are shared with the younger generation. The transmission of values from one generation to another has been taking place orally as well as through written texts, over the ages. In the modern world different mass communication media have taken up this function.

(7) Entertainment: To break the monotony of human life, we need to be exposed to art, literature, music, films, dance, drama, sports and other modes of entertainment. Communication provides us with this necessary diversion. Thus entertainment is an equally important function of communication. However, of late, this element has overtaken other functions especially in various mass communication media. Some television news channels are found to be biased towards entertainment value rather than informational content of a news item. Similarly, cable and satellite television channels are dishing out inane programmes in the name of entertainment. There is a need to strike a judicious balance between the different needs of the audience enabling them to take advantage of the wealth of information on various issues rather than succumbing to the dictates of cheap entertainment.

Q2.What are the models of communication? Explain briefly each of them.

Ans. A model is representation of some reality. It can be any object, event, happening, a process or an activity. According to Mortensen, "In broadest sense, a model is a systematic representation of an object or event in idealised in abstract form. Models are somewhat arbitrary by nature. The act of abstracting the reality eliminates certain details to focus on essential factors. The key to the usefulness of a model is the degree to which it conforms in point by point correspondence to the underlying determinants of communication behaviour. In this way, models allow us to see one thing in terms of another. By examining models, one learns not only about the object, situation or process, but also about perspective of the designer.

The communication models try to clarify the nature of communication. They try to provide simplified explanation of the complex dynamics to help us to understand the components and process involving the communication behaviour. They also provide important insights into perspective of the designers.

Types of Communication Models: There are many models of communication. Some important models of communication are given below:

(1) Lasswell's Model of Communication: Horald D. Lasswell was one of the famous scholars who provided a classical model for the explanation of the process and mechanism of communication. He mentioned five components comprising a communication process. His model implies that more than one channel can carry a message. The "Who" raises the question of control of messages; "Says what" is the subject of content analysis; "To whom" deals with receivers and audience; and "With what effect" relates to credibility of the message as well as the status of the receiver. However, the graphic idea of his model can be seen as follows:

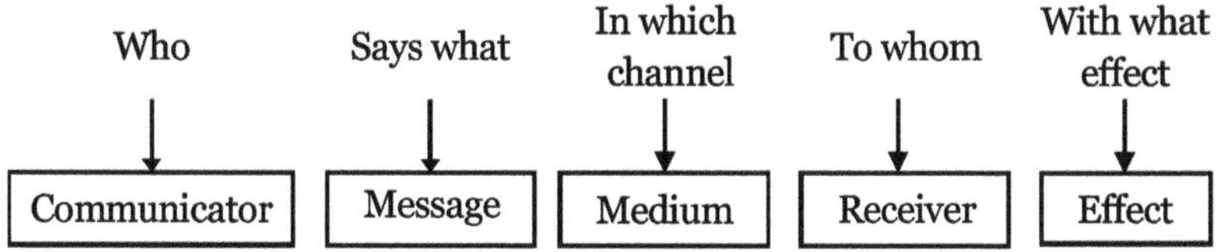

Fig. 1.1: Graphic Idea of the Lasswell's Model

(2) Shannon Weaver Information Model: In 1949, Claude E. Shannon and Warren Weaver proposed a communication model. They believed that their model characterised communication in a very general way. According to this model, the speaker selects a desired message from all the possible messages. The message is send through a communication channel and changed into signals (messages). The receiver receives the signals. In the process of transmission, certain distortions get added which are not the part of the message sent by the source. They called this noise.

This model led to the technical improvements in the message transmissions and attracted scholars from several disciplines to study communication scientifically. Their effort was towards developing a unified model of communication. The focus of this model was on three components, viz. channel noise, semantic noise and feedback. These three components were considered for the first time in the communication process. Channel noise suggested any interference with the transmission of the message. Semantic noise occurs when message is misunderstood. Feedback is the third component to assess the 'effects' and comprehend the intended message adequately.

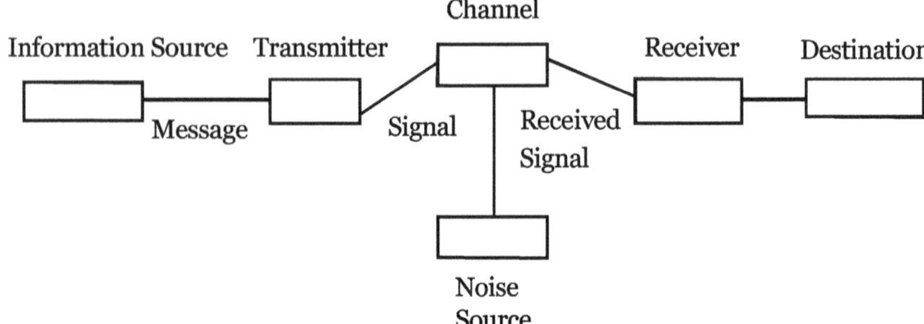

Fig. 1.2: Shannon Weaver Information Model

(3) Charles Osgood's Model (1954): It does not follow the conventional pattern of communication from source to channel to receiver. He describes communication as a dynamic process and says that a given communication event may begin with receiving stimuli as shown below:

Osgood stressed that each participant in the communication process sends as well as receives messages and as such encodes, decodes, and interprets messages. Thus, according to Osgood, communication is a dynamic process in which there is an interactive relationship between the source and the receiver where a person may be a source one moment, a receiver the next and again a source the following moment. This is particularly true in interpersonal communication.

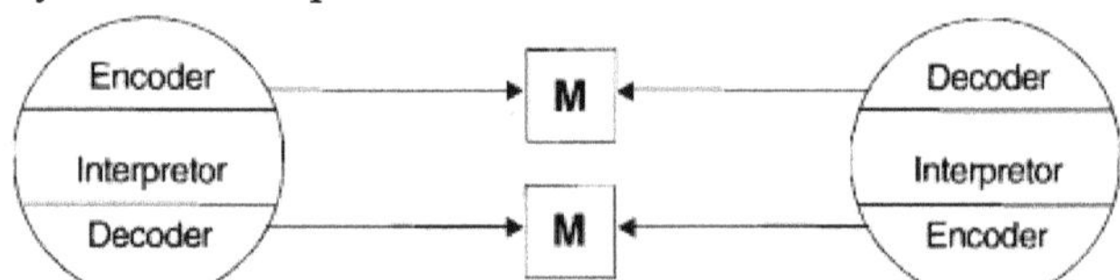

Fig. 1.3: Charles Osgood's Model

Schramm Model (1954): Wilbur Lang Schramm began studying communication as a separate discipline altogether and developed a model which had a unique feature of involving 'field of experience' of the sender and the receiver Schramm's model 1954 is a derivation from the Shannon and Weaver model but emphasizes on the process of encoding and decoding.

Schramm opines messages become complicated because of the different meanings learned by different people. Meanings can be connotative and denotative. Connotative meanings are emotional and based on personal experiences which may vary with varying experiences. Denotative meanings are dictionary meanings which usually remain unaltered when received by people. He further adds that messages have surface and latent meanings which might be interpreted differently. Besides, pitch pattern, modulation of voice, facial expressions also might be conceived differently by different people. He opines communication is the process of establishing commonness or oneness of thought between a sender and a receiver. In order that the information sent by the sender is understood by the receiver they must have a common 'field of experience'. Figure will help to illustrate the concept of field of experience

The sender encodes the message based on his understanding and experience, i.e. on the whole his field of experience. Thereafter this encoded message gets conveyed to the receiver. The receiver now, interprets the message in the background of his field of experience. The degree, to which the message is decoded in the manner it was intended by the encoder, depends on the degree or extent of commonality in the fields of the encoder and the decoder. So, more the two fields overlap, more will be the understanding. For example, a lecture on neuron physiologically will either make little or no sense if delivered to fifth standard school kids. This would happen because the lecturer's knowledge about biology or chemistry is no way common to the experience of the school kids, neither are they likely to have knowledge of the vocabulary used for the purpose.

Also, this model is an interactional model and introduces the idea of feedback from the receiver to the sender. The receiver does send back feedback to the sender thus making communication a continuous process.

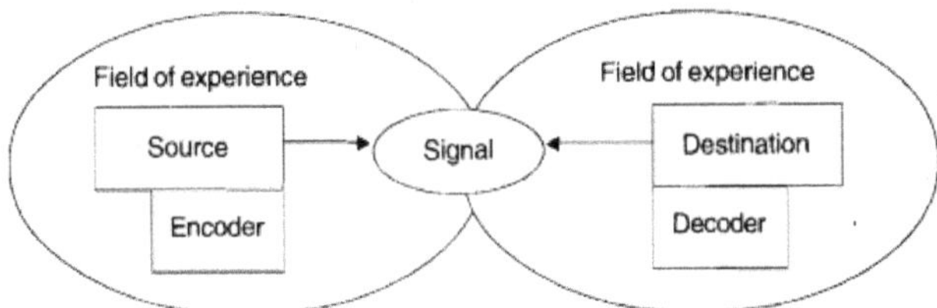

Fig. 1.4: Schramm Model

Q3. Briefly describe the process of communication.

Ans. The communication process is made up of four key components. Those components include encoding, medium of transmission, decoding and feedback. There are also two other factors in the process, and those two factors are present in the form of the sender and the receiver. The communication process begins with the sender and ends with the receiver. The process of communication has four major elements. These elements are sender (source), message (idea), channel (through which message propagate) and receiver (target). However, another major element of communication is feedback. Students study these elements to understand the type of interrelationship that exists among them and what parts they play in communication process. These are discussed as follows:

- **Sender:** Sender is a person who sends the message. A sender makes use of symbols (words, graphic, or visual aids) to convey the message and produce the required response. For instance, a training manager conducting training for new batch of employees. Sender may be an individual, a group, or an organisation. The views, background, approach, skills, competencies and knowledge of the sender have a great impact on the message. The verbal and non-verbal symbols chosen are essential in ascertaining interpretation of the message by the recipient in the same terms as intended by the sender.
- **Message:** Message is a key idea that the sender wants to communicate. It is a sign that elicits the response of recipient. Communication process begins with deciding about the message to be conveyed, therefore, it must be ensured that the main objective of the message is clear.

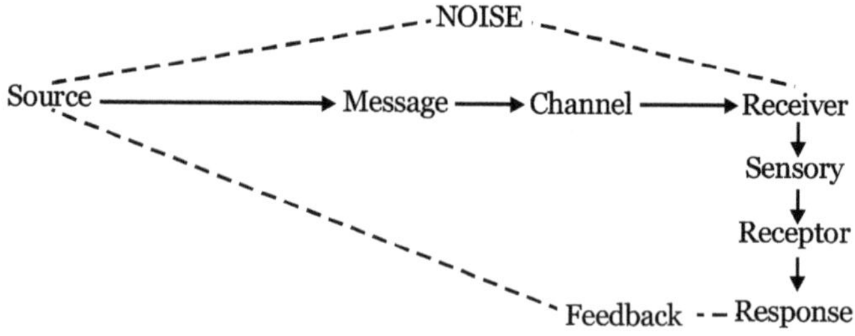

Fig. 1.5: Elements of Communication

- **Channel:** Channel is a means used to exchange/transmit the message. The sender must choose an appropriate channel for transmitting the message. The choice of appropriate channel of communication is essential for making the message effective and correctly interpreted by the recipient. This choice of communication medium varies depending upon the features of communication. For instance, written medium is chosen when a message has to be conveyed to a small group of people, while an oral medium is chosen when spontaneous feedback is required from the recipient as misunderstandings are cleared immediately.
- **Receiver:** Receiver is a person for whom the message is intended/aimed/targeted. The degree to which the receiver understands the message is dependent upon various factors such as knowledge of recipient, their responsiveness to the message, and the reliance of encoder on decoder.
- **Feedback:** Feedback is the main component of communication process as it permits the sender to analyse the efficacy of the message. It helps the sender in confirming the correct interpretation of message by the decoder. Feedback may be verbal (through words) or non-verbal (in form of smiles, sighs, etc.). It may also be taken in written form (through memos, reports, etc).
- **Noise:** It can be referred as the distortion in communication of message upto the receiver's end. Noise can be occurred internally or externally. It also creates many types of barriers in communication. It have many implications in the process of communication.

Q4. What are the types of communication?

Ans. There are following types of communication can be determined among teachers and learners:

(1) Interpersonal Communication: Interpersonal communication happens between two persons the sender and receiver, who in an educational setting could be the teacher and the learner. The learner is not necessarily the receiver and may also be the sender when s/he questions, opines, responds, i.e. interacts. Various sensory channels (sense organs) are used for receiving the information. Visualizing includes watching the facial expressions, gestures, and body language of each other. Similarly, hearing involves attaching meaning to the words/sounds communicated and also making out the tone, pith, and other things related to the delivery of messages. This helps in gauging the inner meaning of the communication. It allows us to clarify our views, persuade or motivate learners more effectively. In this type of communication the scope for misunderstanding and doubts is minimised and clarity of views is facilitated.

(2) Group Communication: A group is formed when we establish interaction bonds with other persons. This type or level of communication takes place within a group. The purpose of group communication is to communicate information that is of common interest to group members or sometimes to know the opinions of group members to arrive at a decision.

Group communication has several strengths when used for education and training. The simplest example of this is the classroom setting where there is sharing of the message (lesson) with the receivers (learners) using a channel of communication (oral/written/visual form). Informing, raising questions and providing answers (feedback) are some of the activities involved in it. The size of the group has implications in the communication process. The element of interactivity existing in interpersonal communication is also present in small group communication which, however, diminishes in large group situations.

(3) Mass Communication: Mass communication is a more public form of communication between an entity and a large and diverse audience, mediated by some form of technology. In mass communication, the source is not an individual, but a formal organisation.

Mass communication media are being increasingly used for the purpose of education and training. It is a means of public communication reaching large audiences. Newspapers, motion pictures, radio, television, and magazines can deliver information to millions of people. To the list of the media we can also add the networking facilities, especially the Internet that reaches huge number of users. Mass media are used when the learner population is widespread, scattered and it is difficult to reach out to them through the face-to-face situations. In distance education a variety of media components are used for communicating with distantly placed learners. Some of these media are: radio broadcasts, telecasts, interactive radio, teleconferencing etc.

(4) Intrapersonal Communication: The word "intra" denotes "within" which means when we communicate within ourselves, it is called intrapersonal communication. This type of communication takes place within a single person when stimuli are received, often for the purpose of clarifying ideas or analysing a situation. Other times, intrapersonal communication is undertaken in order to reflect upon or appreciate something. It is also known as information processing. For example, when we see a good crop, we may share our joy with some person if one is around otherwise we keep our joy to ourselves, thinking how lucky we are and so on.

It is especially useful for contemplating, visualising and analysing in the context of education and training. It helps the communicator i.e. the teacher to plan a message carefully. Some teachers take great pains to plan their lectures/presentations by spending considerable time in organising their ideas, thoughts and approaches to communicate them effectively. They visualise their learners, refine their ideas and use appropriate vocabulary to express their views. If we read a book, watch a film, use audio-visual aids and reflect over the content and production aspects and analyse them, these can be placed under intra-personal communication. The degree of intra-personal communication may, however, vary from one person to another. It may trigger off great creativity in some while it may not be so profound in others.

Q5. What are the barriers which hinder the smooth flow of communication?

Ans. Any type of hindrances in communication can deter the flow of communication. In this situation message cannot reach at its desired location or form upto the receiver end. These barriers have been discussed below:

- **Physical Barriers:** Often learners are not comfortable with the source of communication which is not visible to them or sometimes with their environment also, it may create barriers in communication. Geographical distance may also create barriers, as people may like to communicate with one another but due to physical distances may not be able to do so. For example, people may be interested to communicate with an expert in a particular area who is not available in other areas/regions as there is physical barrier.

- **Psychological Barriers:** As different people have various thoughts likes and dislikes as their individual differences, attitudes and motivation levels, we make them to perceive things and situations differently. Apart from this, the varied levels of anxiety, inherent prejudices and previous experiences also create barriers in communication. Studies have revealed that due to the process of selective perception, selective recall and selective retention, we perceive, retain as well as recall a message selectively thus creating barriers in communication.
- **Socio-cultural Barriers:** In communication process there is also have socio-cultural barriers. For instance, in the Indian context, some women may not like to discuss their health related problem with a male health worker. Similarly, some issues may be perceived as personal and not fit for discussion outside the realm of family, thus creating barriers. Some societies are less vocal which may affect their level of communication with those from other cultures who are more vocal or aggressive in behaviour.
- **Linguistic Barriers:** For communication, during the process of communication, faulty expressions, poor translation, verbosity, ambiguous words and inappropriate vocabulary create barriers. Moreover, words and symbols used to communicate facts and information may mean different things to different persons. This is due to the fact that meanings are in the minds of people who perceive and interpret meanings in different ways according to their individual frame of mind.
- **Technical Barriers:** Technology becomes the essential part of communication but sometimes using technology, technical barriers also make the process of communication complex. When audio quality is poor or video signals are weak, the message may not clearly reach the target group. Erratic power supply also creates barriers in communication.
- **Barriers Due to Information Load:** At times too much information is imparted which we may not able to

comprehend and assimilate, thus creating a barrier in communication. To illustrate, in a meeting when a speaker provides information at a fast pace for considerable period of time many of the issues and concepts may get lost at the end. While using media, this type of barrier can greatly affect the level of comprehension and utilisation of the message. Hence, great care needs to be taken while deciding the amount of information in a communication transaction.

Q6. Write the strategies which are effective for communication.

Ans. Communication strategy in education technology is designed to help learners and teachers to communicate effectively and meet core educational objectives. For an effective communication, there are following objects are in need:

- **Clarity of message:** In any type of communication, it is important that the objective of communication is well defined, the level of language is kept simple, brief and clear. It has been found that most of the complex ideas can be presented simply. Short and simple sentences can express an idea completely, coherently and cogently. Too many conjunctions make a sentence complex and difficult to understand. Proper phrasing, punctuation, emphasis, voice modulation facilitates clarity of message and increases the impact of communication.
- **Reinforcement of ideas:** For clarity of the message, an element of redundancy needs to be introduced. Difficult or technical words and expressions need to be substituted with simpler expressions and words of everyday usage. However, care needs to be taken to see that the message does not become repetitive and boring. The level of audience needs to be constantly kept in mind.
- **Appropriate channel:** Depending upon the type and objective of communication, selection of appropriate channel is crucial for the success of communication. The use of technology also helps to overcome geographical barriers. However, for selecting a particular channel, especially the more expensive one, some questions need to be constantly asked such as why this channel? Is there any specific need? Will it help to meet the objective of communication? Is it possible to avoid unnecessary

investment? and so on. Many a time, a simple channel may convey a message more effectively as compared to the more glamorous ones.

- **Motivation:** Motivation also helps to remove some of the barriers, especially psychological and socio-cultural barriers. The receivers in the communication process need to be encouraged to express their views, opinions and doubts. They need to be drawn into the interactive process by persuading them to pose questions. Appreciation of their (receivers) views increases their self-esteem and builds confidence.
- **Proper environment:** Proper seating arrangements, visibility of the source and relatively comfortable environment facilitate communication. This is especially conducive in overcoming some of the physical barriers discussed above.
- **Feedback:** Feedback is an important component of any communication activity. Regular feedback at appropriate levels facilitates understanding of the needs and views of the receiver/s. It helps to bridge the gaps, if any, in the communication approach and improves the process of communication.

Q7. What do you mean by educational communication? Describe the nature of educational communication in brief.

Ans. Educational communication can be defined as the communication among teachers and learners but this communication can be of two types one is classroom communication and another one is distance learning communication through printed and audio-visual based materials.

Besides educational purpose we need communication for information and entertainment. Where communication is limited to sensitisation on various issues. But in educational technology or for educational purpose, communication should meet the following two broad criteria:

- It should aim to improve the learning of recipients in some kind of permanent way.
- It should explore the subject or develop a treatment of it in a systematic and organized way.

For achieving above mentioned criteria we need to explore the nature of educational communication in following way:

(1) Purposive nature: This nature of educational communication allows the source, that could be the teacher, to share information with learners for a variety of purposes. These could be related to creation of knowledge, stretch mental horizons, and raise levels of aspirations. Communication is also meant to focus attention on problems having a bearing on the contemporary developmental and educational context; it can encourage experimentation and knowledge relating to their success and/or failure can be widely disseminated. It may aimed at developing a certain attitude to build a set of values. It may be related with building of tastes and appreciation of arts or literature. Thus educational communication has a definite purpose to accomplish as per the needs of the target group (learners).

(2) Positive nature: For the completion of teaching-learning object we can use the positive nature of educational communication. Positive nature confirms the surety of good result. It contributes to the harmonious integration of the individuals in society. It can be effectively employed to build consensus on new goals, for promoting understanding of an issue or taking positive action.

(3) Pragmatic Nature: A single technique could not be appropriate for the education and training. We need to apply both theoretical and practical techniques for achieving the purpose of educational communication. Pragmatic Nature may be related with certain changes in the learners' behaviour, leading to development of specific skills and techniques or showing them how to carry out a particular process. Debates, argumentation and public speaking are examples of pragmatic nature of communication as they influence or facilitate decision-making.

Q8. Write short notes on following:

(i) Contagious and non-contagious communication

Ans. In contiguous communication, the communicator, who in educational communication happens to be the teacher is in touch with receivers, i.e. learners and the communication process takes place in an unbroken sequence. Contiguous communication allows proximity between sender and receiver/s. Classroom communication, and individual instructions in the formal education system can be placed under contiguous communication. However, for reaching out to a large number of learners, it can prove to be time consuming and expensive as they have to be physically present. That in turn requires adequate infrastructure. This can be done not only in the face-to-face mode but also through chat sessions, use of conferencing facilities over electronic media, etc.

In non-contiguous communication, the sequence of communication is broken and the communicator (teacher) is not in direct touch with the receivers (learners). When large number of dispersed learners are being reached with the help of different media such as radio, television, computers, Internet etc. and there is no direct touch between the teacher and the learners, and the sequence in communication is broken, it can be categorised as non-contiguous communication. This is being increasingly used for teaching core curriculum based subjects. For instance, learning from the print material that you are presently undertaking is an example of this type of communication.

(2) Synchronous and Asynchronous Communication: In synchronous communication, the participants in the communication activity are present in real time at same and/or different locations. Classroom teaching, face-to-face tutorials, workshops, radio and television broadcasts, audio conferencing, video conferencing, telephonic calls, etc. can be placed in this category. Synchronous communication may also include text based chat, i.e. chat over the Internet with communication in real time through text between two or more people and audio chat.

Asynchronous communication does not require the simultaneous presence of participants to provide two-way communication at a distance. In asynchronous communication, the teacher and the learner do not meet face-to-face in real time but can be in touch through technology at the user's convenience. Participants can contribute at their own pace and convenient times by carefully reflecting over the information given. In asynchronous communication, information can be edited, stored and retrieved. This type of communication allows a greater degree of freedom and flexibility to the learners. Letters, electronic mail, mailing lists, bulletin boards, discussion groups in which participants can exchange and respond to open messages, fall under this category. Asynchronous communication may be difficult and time consuming, yet it has been found to be pedagogically effective.

(3) Direct and Mediated Communication: In a traditional teaching situation, the teacher is in direct contact with his/her students. S/he presents the topic, explains the content, guides and encourages the students. The students in turn also know how to interpret the messages, expressions, body language and variations of tone, etc. of the teacher. Since there is no medium to carry the messages between the teacher and the learner, this type of communication is said to be direct. Sometimes face-to-face pedagogic communication is associated with non-mediated communication. However, some scholars have argued that no knowledge can exist nor be expressed without some kind of symbolic representation such as the use of language.

When we teach indirectly and get in touch with learners through varied communication means, it is known as mediated communication. In this type of communication, when the teacher teaches offline, the students need not be present at the same time or at the same place. The contents can be shared with the learner through various media such as printed course materials, audio-visual programmes and other information and communication technologies like the networked computers. Distance education system makes extensive use of mediated communication, which is at the core of teaching-learning process.

Q9. Write a short note on electronic communication.

Ans. As communication is old of ages, but electronic communication is comparatively younger than other modes of communication.

The communication is concerned with electronic equipment used for the transfer of information between two or more points. That information may be voice, television pictures, computer data, or some other form of electronic information.

Besides all above mentioned mediums electronic communication rigidly stands for communication through internet. It is also known as e-communication or online communication.

Internet constitutes the backbone of online communication which is being used extensively for educational purposes. The Internet facilitates educational communication by connecting communities of learners and teachers as well as other knowledge seekers and facilitates communication through emails, chats, and other services on the World Wide Web (WWW). Real time interaction is possible using audio video communication, texts, graphics, images, animation, etc. In sharp contrast to the direct teaching approach, the instructional approach of online learning lets the students 'act' rather than 'listen'. It facilitates collaborative learning, mentoring via apprenticeships and learning by doing. It also fosters learner autonomy and thus facilitates individualised learning.

Communication through e-mail: E-mail is an electronic message sent from one computer to another over the Internet. This can be done either in the form of message or with attachments, pictures and other documents. In the context of education, it is an excellent means of communication with dispersed sender/receiver. You might have used e-mails and noticed that like postal letters, e-mails also contain two parts: header and body. Header contains the name, address of the sender, the subject of the message, etc. and the body contains the message itself.

E-mails can be used effectively for educational communication but we need to follow some etiquette. This is known as Netiquettes. First of all e-mail needs to be sent to the person who really needs to be contacted, otherwise it is known as SPAM or unsolicited mail. The subject line should clearly indicate what the e-mail is about. The message should be short and focused. Since e-mails can be intercepted and read by others or forwarded accidentally, one should avoid writing information, which is very personal and sensitive in nature. One should take time to think and frame the proper e-mail, check the spellings before sending the mails as mis-spelt mails create a poor impression on the recipient. One should avoid using all capital letters as it makes reading more difficult, this is known as SHOUTING. For optimal utilisation, user should check e-mails regularly and the unwanted ones should be deleted periodically.

Q10. Discuss the role of communication for educational training.

Ans. There is a dire need of communication for educational training for teachers because training is an ongoing process which is aimed at acquiring competencies and skills for doing a particular job. The main purpose of training is to bridge the gap between job requirements and the competence of a trainee. In the modern competitive environment, and rapid rate of obsolescence, training acquires great importance.

The objectives of training are specific and utilitarian: Training can be provided through various methods. These are as follows:

(1) Workshop is a practical session in which trainees learn by doing various exercises. During workshop, a group of people get together to

work on a creative project and the emphasis is on 'doing' rather than on theory. It is designed to illustrate the application of theoretical principles. In a workshop the trainees undertake certain activities individually or in groups.

(2) Induction/orientation programmes are organised for new employees or students. These are generally for short duration to orient them into a specific area earmarked for training. It makes the person familiar with the nature of the job or an educational programme in which s/he has enrolled and his/her role in it.

(3) Lecture method is the simplest and the oldest method of instruction. The knowledge in a particular area on a topic, not readily available to group members is to be imparted by an expert. It is useful for teaching conceptual knowledge to a large group in a short span of time. It is primarily a one-way mode of communication. However, a good lecture involves effective interaction between the instructor and the trainees through the use of good questions followed by explanations. Thus there is two way communication.

(4) Discussion is a planned activity in which a small number of trainees get together and discuss a topic. At times a moderator who keeps the discussion focused on the issue guides them. For using discussion as a training method, the topic selected generally has adequate scope of generating divergent views.

(5) Debate fosters collaborative learning. In this method, trainees are divided into two groups. One person from each group is asked to speak for and against the problem. The group members have to defend their arguments and convince the other group.

(6) Internship also entails learning by doing at workplace for a specific period. This is generally organised for advance students for undergoing supervised practical training. Candidates go through their regular studies and also work to acquire practical knowledge and skills.

(7) Brainstorming focuses on a specific problem or an issue and a group of participants pull out ideas in an informal manner. This method does not place emphasis on right or wrong answers but on a free flow of ideas that may be novel, original and may even initially appear unusual. All the possible aspects are recorded, evaluated and selected at the end of the brainstorming.

(8) Apprenticeship provides a person opportunity to learn a trade by working for an agreed period and get both theoretical as well as practical training. An apprentice is a person who works under a skilled or qualified person in order to learn a trade or programme for a recognised period. It teaches correct job methods and develops confidence in job performance.

In addition to above mentioned methods there are many other methods of training such as study visits to professional organisations expose the participants to the working in a particular organisation. Buzz sessions allow each member of the group to express his/her opinion during a specific time allotted. Demonstration reveals a particular process in a step-by-step systematic manner. Role-play method allows the learners to enact different roles in an imaginary situation on a problem or issue concerning them. Case study method focuses on a problem or situation and the trainees analyse the problem in depth and suggest remedial measures. Communication is at the heart of each of these training methods.

Q11. Describe, how planning communication for education and training can be done.

Ans. (1) Know Your Learners: In the process of planning communication for education and training it is important to know the level and needs of the learners. The socio-demographic profile, educational background and dynamics of the learners also need to be kept in mind. Despite the overt homogeneity, they may be a heterogeneous lot due to different socio-economic levels, different ideologies, abilities, and sensitivities. This makes the process of communication complex and challenging.

While planning the content, a balanced and holistic view combining different facets of an issue will help to develop critical thinking among the varied learners. In addition, the existing level of knowledge of the students, their learning needs, and learning styles provide information about the strategies for communication. Knowledge about their values, attitudes and cultural background helps the teacher in placing them in proper context. An assessment of their motivation and desire to learn helps to plan the message accordingly.

(2) Proper Organisation of Context: In planning communication once topic or subject of communication has been identified, utmost care needs to be taken while structuring the content, e.g. lesson plans. It needs to be broken into segments and each segment should be sequenced properly in a logical manner. The entire effort should be geared so that learner is able to understand the message and add to his/her knowledge. While selecting the content, care needs to be taken to ensure that it is factual as any mistake can lead to a series of misinformation.

In addition, it should be updated regularly in view of the rapid pace of obsolescence in some areas of knowledge. It should be focused and specific and should not lead to generalities. It should be adequately supplemented with illustrations, examples and case studies for explaining a phenomenon.

(3) Selection of appropriate Topic: The topic on which communication has to be made should be important and relevant for the target group. It should be interesting enough for the receiver (learner) to motivate him/her and sustain his/her attention. Conscious efforts need to be made to provide adequate scope for eliciting different viewpoints so that the process of communication does not become a one-way monologue and is able to involve others.

(4) Setting Realistic Goals: Since educational communication is purposive and pragmatic in nature, there are certain learning outcomes (goals), which have to be achieved at the end of communication transaction.

The source (teacher) should be very clear about the aim of communication. The objectives should be specific, setting out what learners should be able to do after completing the act of educational communication. Putting too much of information in one communication transaction will lead to boredom, fatigue and lack of attention. The fact that our attention span is limited also places a great deal of constraint on the source while planning and designing objectives. At the same time, less information will leave room for doubts and require clarification. Well defined objectives can provide a basis for assessment later on.

(5) Appropriate Duration: The duration of educational transaction also affects communication. When a teacher imparts a lengthy discourse or a long presentation is made which is not interactive or does not give breaks in terms of the use of teaching/visual aids, this may create a barrier. Studies have revealed that human mind can effectively receive information for a span of 55 minutes to one hour at a stretch and after that the level of attention starts waning. Information overload leads to saturation and fatigue. The longer the message the concentration starts decreasing and inability to concentrate.

(6) Selection of Technology: Selection of technology for education should be made with utmost care. In our search for new inventions and their applications for education, we have to be extremely careful about their implications in learning. We need to constantly ask, questions such as: Do learners have access to this media? Is the use of a particular medium justified? Can it be done in a simpler way? Will a particular medium actually facilitate learning? An honest appraisal of the answers to such questions should govern the selection of a particular media. The tendency to use technology as a fashionable trend has to be eschewed. The famous poet, T.S.Eliot has once said, "Where is the wisdom we have lost in knowledge? Where is the knowledge we have lost in information" In our scramble for using technology for education and training, we might end up giving information without either the knowledge or the wisdom that could be derived out of it.

Q12. What are the types of communication skills? Describe in your own words.

Ans. The purpose of communication is to convey the message across to the recipient(s) clearly and unambiguously. Otherwise the message may be misinterpreted resulting in confusions. Communication is successful when both the sender and the receiver interpret the information in the same manner during communication. Therefore for purposeful communication, there are needed skills. These skills can be discussed as follows:

(1) Listening Skills: Listening is must for imparting education or any information because attentive listening is a prerequisite of good communication. A successful communication also involves good listeners, critics, followers and respondents. Skilled listeners are valued, as during a communication process, usually all the participants are eager to have their say or find it difficult to concentrate on the source. For effective communication, it is extremely important that the sender and receivers listen to each other attentively. In our daily conversations you would have noticed that most of us like to express our views and can talk at length on any issue, but very few people turn out to be good listeners. A good communicator puts the listeners at ease, s/he stops talking once in a while and invites views and opinions of others and concentrates on what is being said. S/he encourages plurality of views, appreciates and accords respects to even those which are contrary to his/her views.

Listening can be at different levels. Initially, we make sense out of sounds to distinguish speaker's words and try to understand what is being said. Then we analyse the point of view of the speaker. At times, our own personal biases may creep in and make the communication process difficult. On other occasions, the tone of the speaker, gestures, postures and facial expressions may contradict what is being said and they could act as barriers to listening. However, mere listening is not enough, it has to be active and emphatic implying that while listening, your mind should be alert and your face and posture should reflect interest in what is being said.

Body postures indicate whether one is listening or drifting away.

(2) Writing Skills: Writing skills is especially relevant while preparing lessons for students, writing chapters for books or contributing research papers for academic journals. While writing, the sender needs to ask if it conveys the message with clarity or creates linguistic or semantic barriers. Is it verbose or is there economy of words? Does it offer scope for clarification and substitution? Are there jumps or breaks which needs to be bridged? Has one concept been explained in totality before moving on to another concept? So, for entertaining these queries one has to own clarity and conciseness

(3) Verbal Skills: In educational communication, the teacher as the source has access to information which needs to be shared with learners. This has to be done effectively so that the recipient i.e. the learner understands as the source intends. Apart from subject specific expertise, the verbal skills of the source greatly affect the process of communication. Verbal skills include felicity with the spoken language, whatever the language may be. The pitch of voice should be neither very high nor low. Well-modulated voice, which is able to convey the varied expressions with appropriate intonation and inflexions add to the ability to convey. In addition, correct pronunciation and proper diction add to the verbal skills of the source. The pace of delivery is also an important factor in verbal skills because if the pace of delivery is too fast, it will be difficult for the learner to assimilate the information.

To address the above issues the sender needs to ask whether the language used is pitched at the right level. Is it appropriate for the level of receivers or is too highbrow which puts them in a daze? Does it move at a fast pace which is receiver is unable to assimilate? All these factors greatly impinge on the success of educational communication.

(4) Questioning Skills: Any communication effort is incomplete, if it is a one-way monologue and does not offer scope for interactivity and feedback. The sender has to be very sure of the fact that the message has been received properly as intended. This can be cross checked by putting questions and assessing the responses. Questions serve as important tools of learning. Teaching by questioning is commonly referred to as the "Socratic Method". It is often the basis of our educational approach. A good question can accomplish this result better than just telling the answer. Think of a situation in which a speaker rambles on and on putting the participants to sleep. All of a sudden an interesting question from the participants captures the interest of the group and brings them back from their reverie.

For effecting educational communication, the skill of asking questions needs to be developed. Questions need to be framed carefully. Ideally questions should be brief, specific and polite. These questions can be direct, leading or rhetorical. After asking a question adequate time needs to be given to students to respond to the question. During prolonged training sessions, conscious efforts are made to build interactive sessions which apart from giving scope for interaction provide a much needed break to the participants.

Q13. Explain briefly, the nature of classroom communication.

Ans. In classroom communication, there are learners and teacher who communicate for the completion of teaching-learning objectives.

It is purposive, positive and pragmatic in nature. It takes place between teacher and learners and among learners both in formal as well as informal situations. It involves speaking, lecturing, describing, explaining, illustrating on the part of the teacher, and engaging the students in debate, dialogue and discussion. Learners raise questions, doubts and queries to make their difficulties explicit which need to be effectively responded to and addressed by the teacher.

The strength of this approach lies in facilitating maximum feedback, warmth, and interaction. However, the limitation is that it is a teacher-centered approach based on the principle of 'teaching by telling' and 'learning by listening' in which the onus of teaching lies on the teacher. It may be noted that despite the presence of a teacher learners may remain passive recipients of information. If they express their disinterest or passivity, an alert teacher can still control it by using various interactive techniques in arousing and sustaining the interest of the students. However, the problem may become acute when despite a student's apparent interest in the lecture/lesson through appropriate facial expressions and body language, his/her mind may wander elsewhere without following what is being discussed in the class.

A teacher has to be a good speaker and at the same time has to be a patient and attentive listener for his/her learners. Active listening is different from just hearing and requires activities such as hearing, understanding, i.e. attaching meaning to what is heard and judging and thinking about it.

Q14. Discuss any three technologies that facilitate classroom teaching.

Ans. Technology has made teaching-learning more comprehensive and learning friendly. As the technology getting advanced, so is our teaching-learning methodology. Now we are using simple teaching aids viz., maps, diagrams, charts, posters, etc. ,with audio-video resources, projectors, computers and so on.

Studies have revealed that if used effectively, technology applications can help students in using higher order thinking skills such as thinking critically, analyzing, making inferences and solving problems. It can involve students in innovative and creative activities in collaborative way. Technology provides access to information and helps in establishing contact with teachers and students located at different locations. Technology in classroom teaching can be discussed as follows:

(1) Audio-Video Resources: Audio-video aids/cassettes can be effectively used in the classroom situation to make learning interesting as well as engaging. Audio cassettes require power supply/batteries, audio tapes and tape recorder while the use of video cassettes in the classroom will require television monitor, VCR and power supply. For using audio-visual resources in a class, the first step would be to identify the material on the subject. The audio resources available both within and outside the school/institution need to be selected. At times, permission to use them also has to be undertaken. After a thorough listening or preview, you have to decide whether the whole programme has to be used in the class or selectively. If selectively, then those portions need to be identified and cued. During teleconferencing sessions audio-video excerpts can be integrated in the design of sessions to highlight some teaching points and also to make the sessions interesting. After listening/viewing of the programme discussion can be built on the issues raised.

Many institutions are investing in simple audio-video gadgets in view of the benefits accrued. For example, if an institution has access to video camera, students can practice speaking in front of an audience. They can develop their video portfolio to demonstrate gradual progress in learning a language or a subject over a period of time.

Many a time, relevant material on a subject may not be readily available and has to be produced. In that case, factors such as willingness of the institution for programme production, resources available in terms of finances, time and personnel at the institutional level, etc. need to be taken into consideration. For using audio-visual resources in the classroom, some basic care is required. First of all, the equipment should be in place and ideally, it should be checked to ensure whether everything is working properly. The functionality of equipment before starting the class should be ensured.

(2) Computer Technology: The access to computers is growing at a steady pace. Computers are largly being used in educational institutions for academic and administrative purposes. The Internet has already captured the imagination of the educational community. It has been found that computer technology can support meaningful, engaged learning for students instead of rote learning. Students can visit the relevant websites and update their knowledge on a given subject. Grades can be upgraded regularly on the school website which can be easily accessed by parents and students alike. Students can get more involved in their studies by monitoring their progress through regular checking of their assignments and grades. Like other forms of technological inputs, the use of computers is generally determined on the basis of its application, i.e. how it is used for learning. The uses of computers in classrooms could be for teaching, exploring, creating, composing, storing, and anlysing data or for communication with others.

The use of computer requires some basic skills, such as operating the computer, word processing through it, preparing slides with power point, etc. Teachers need to be equipped with these skills so that they can access, search, interpret and synthesize information

(3) OHP: OHP or the overhead projector is one of the most commonly used teaching aids in classroom teaching. For using an OHP, slides or transparencies need to be prepared. The first step in this regard would be to select the topic on which you want to develop slides. After proper research, sifting and sieving, content needs to be identified. Then it should be broken into smaller segments maintaining a logical sequencing of the ideas. Each slide should be linked with the next slide to follow. The font size should ideally be 24 or 28 depending upon the size of the class. These slides should be neatly written or word-processed and should not contain many details. One should provide the detailed information during the course of presentation.

You may require technical help for placing the OHP and sharpening the focus on white-board or wall. If handouts of slides have to be distributed, these need to be photocopied and sets prepared in advance. In this case, students can be asked not to take notes, as handouts will be distributed. Some common problems being faced while using OHP are: information overload making the slides cluttered and unreadable, poor focus and power failure among others. Use of OHP slides can complement or supplement the information being communicated by the teacher. However the students remain passive viewers &/ listeners while this technology is used.

Q15. What is the role of a teacher in planning classroom communication?

Ans. In planning classroom communication, the role of a teacher is on apex. For performing his/her responsibility of planning communication, a teacher should be well equipped with facts of the subject to be taught. In addition to meeting the needs of average learners s/he has also to satisfy the intellectual needs of bright students and for that s/he has to be well prepared. S/he has to encourage creativity and innovative approaches so that students bring forth their arguments with appropriate reasoning in contrast with rote learning. S/he also needs to inculcate proper values among the students to enable them to face the economic, social and cultural challenges lying ahead and all these call upon the skills of communication of the teacher. However, a teacher also performs following duties for planning classroom communication:

(1) Developing Classroom Culture: For effective functioning of a class, a harmonious culture needs to be developed and the importance of according respect to the viewpoint of the other should be encouraged. The class set-up should be kept democratic in which the teacher is accorded due respect. It will be difficult to teach if students talk constantly as no one will be able to hear each other. Similarly, communication may not be democratic if a section of vocal learners dominate the interaction whereas shy and timid students do not open up unless specifically drawn. At times, assertive male students may dominate the class at the expense of female students or those from less vocal cultures. Interjecting frequently, talking loudly and shouting, etc. should be discouraged and curbed at all costs.

(2) Developing Communication Skills in Learners: Students need to be encouraged to express their opinions and views or share doubts to develop their reasoning skills and faculties. They should be able to argue, challenge, analyse, and defend ideas. For seeking clarification they can ask: 'could you please repeat the point you just made?', 'I am still not sure if I got it right'. 'could you guide me once again please?' Rephrasing has been found to be an effective method of questioning and they can restate or rephrase what they have heard to clarify certain points.

Communication may also involve trying to look beyond what is said and ascertain what is not said and/or what the missing links in the communication transaction were. Non-verbal cues also convey meanings. For example, if the teacher shuffles the papers or looks away, this may give the impression that student's comments are not taken seriously. Maintaining eye contact, smiling, nodding, etc. help to connect with students. At times, conscious efforts need to be made to maintain eye contact with those who are shy and timid and do not participate freely. For effective learning it is necessary that learners be able to communicate what they know. The teachers need to encourage communication through discussions in the classroom and ensure that every student has understood the communication.

(3) Design and Presentation: In classroom communication there is a need to define the objective of communication clearly and realistically so that these can be met within the specified timeframe. Based on these objectives, message or content needs to be designed which could be verbal, written, pictorial and/or symbolic. The verbal message involves direct communication in the form of lectures, presentations, speeches, etc. Written message includes published information in the form of books, research papers, slides, handouts, etc. Pictorial message includes drawings, graphs, etc. while symbolic messages are used in subjects like Mathematics, Chemistry, Physics, etc. At times rhetorical messages are also used in classroom communication. Rhetoric means the art of oration which includes skills in speaking at length with wit, humour, force and strength.

The message should be simple, lucid, and clear and delivered in an interesting manner in any form of communication. The message should be relevant, updated and pitched at the right level. It is often seen that in our effort to share our knowledge and expertise, we pitch our message at a very high level which may confuse the learner. At times, we may express our biases and prejudices which need to be strongly eschewed. Apart from being free from any type of bias, the message should be credible and persuasive enough to facilitate learner participation. Many a time during the course of a rambling monotonous lecture, one should have to make efforts to keep his/her voice modulation, facial expressions, body language have to be used in facilitating communication.

Q16. What do you mean by the word interactivity?

Or

Define the nature of interactivity in your own words.

Ans. The word "interactivity" refers to that extent to which something is interactive. The dictionary defines interactivity as a reciprocally active process allowing two-way flow of information between the source and the receiver. In other words, interactivity is mainly due to the special attribute of the channel through which communication takes place. According to some authors interactivity is the index of the control and the level of participation of the participants in a communication process. Interactivity may be a feature of face to face communication or of mediated communication. Certain technologies permit more interactivity than others as for instance, technologies facilitating conferencing allow interaction among participants. During interactive communication, messages sent and received are related to each other. The participants thus exercise control over the entire process of communication and especially the content being communicated.

Nature of Interactivity: Interactivity also means face to face communication or of mediated communication interactivity is a condition of communication in which there is simultaneous exchange of message with continuous feedback.

Interactivity is not something to be exclusively associated with technology. It is about people and about experience. It has been found that passivity and interactivity in a communication are qualities of individuals making use of media rather than being the qualities of the media per se. The experiences, perception, outlook and the skills of the participants are some of the important aspects influencing interactivity. What can be inferred is that interactivity goes beyond two-way communication and merges 'speaking' with 'listening' in which simultaneous exchange occurs and feedback is taken into account. It may involve higher level of engagement as compared to communication. It encompasses both intimate person-to-person, face-to-face communication and mediated communication. Interactivity should not be confused with mere technology or navigation facility from one site to another site or from one page to another, as one cannot ensure effective learning by quantity of interactions or by user control especially when that control is limited to mere navigation.

Q17. Discuss the role of interactivity in the teaching-learning process.

Ans. Interactivity can be referred as the backbone of any form of communication and even more for educational communication. Interactivity between teacher and learner has always been regarded as an important element in learning that enables learners to raise questions, seek clarifications, provide instant feedback and come to a "common field of experience". Proper integration and use of interactive multimedia in education can help smooth the path to instructional enlightenment because it can, among other things, provide effective communication, clarify, concepts and enhance teaching and learning via the natural multisensory and intuitive approach. Therefore, our task as instructors and trainers, is to sort, absorb, understand and utilise these new technologies to optimise teaching, training and learning. Interactivity plays following roles in teaching-learning process:

Reduced learning time: According to some research, interactive multimedia/ videodisc training can reduce training time up to 60% over traditional classroom methods. This can be attributed to the immediate interaction and constant feedback which provides excellent reinforcement of concepts and content. Also, self paced instruction which allows students to control the pace and content of their learning i.e., more difficult concepts can be repeated or familiar content can be skipped.

- **Reduced Cost:** The cost of interactive multimedia lie in the design and production. When the same program is used by more students, the cost per student is reduced, unlike the traditional instructional system which needs to cater to teacher salaries and overheads regardless of the number of students.
- **Instructional Consistency and Fairness:** Instructional quality and quantity are not compromised as technology based interactive instruction is consistent and reliable.
- **Increased Retention:** The interactive approach provides a strong learning reinforcement and therefore boosts content retention over time.
- **Mastery of Learning:** A good interactive system can ensure the learning of the prerequisites by learners before proceeding to new content. This provides a strong foundation for continued learning and therefore helps to achieve mastery learning.
- **Increased Motivation:** Immediate feedback and personal control over the content provided by an interactive multimedia system has proven to be highly motivating to learners.
- **More Interactive Learning:** Interactive systems enable learners to have more responsibility and better control over their learning and this generates a greater interest to actively seek new knowledge rather than passively accept instruction.
- **Increased Safety:** Interactive multimedia and the simulations they provide, allow the safe study of hazardous phenomena such as dangerous scientific experiments on harmful substances or natural disasters like volcanic eruptions or earthquakes by the learners.
- **Privacy/accommodates Individual Learning Styles:** This system allows for one to one learning and caters to the different learning styles of individuals. The freedom to ask

questions repeatedly without embarrassment and the involvement of each individual learner motivates them and reduces the potential for distraction.

- **Flexibility:** The flexibility comes from the ability to navigate, by using a keyboard, mouse or touch screen, through an interactive program and to choose what and how much information we want and when we want it.

Q18. List different levels of interaction.

Ans. Interactivity may be at different levels that determine the degree of control of the learners over the content and structure of a programme. These are as follows:

- **Reactive:** In reactive interaction, users react to a given subject matter in ways which have been predetermined by the courseware designer. As for instance, the learner could read a frame (small section of content), stop and read the questions, answer them and then look for feedback. These interactions are usually limited and carried out under directions, rather than being the outcome of reflection on the part of the learner. Reactive designs are thus restrictive and closed as the interactions are forced rather than need based and spontaneous.
- **Proactive:** In proactive interaction, the learner takes the initiative to build up a dialogue. The learner reflects on the content and creatively comes out with responses and queries. The interaction is thus not of closed or limited type. It empowers the learner with greater control over the content and its delivery.
- **Coactive:** This is in between the earlier two types and the users' interaction is based upon the choices of the learner but only to a certain extent.

  Interactivity can also be classified as low, medium and high level. In low level interactivity as for instance in a lecture, interactivity could be low, unless there is a conscious attempt to build it. However there can seldom be a teacher who totally disallows interactivity. A lecture delivered through radio or TV without the facility for interaction could be an example of this. Teaching can also involve medium interactivity as for instance in computer assisted learning where the computer can answer but only through the massage included in the programme. There cannot be creative responses or questions. In high level interactions the source and the recipients interact freely and creatively.

The freedom to interact can enhance the level of alertness and facilitates active participation among learners. Difficult terms, vagueness and ambiguity in presentations can be identifies and suitably corrected. Thus interactivity can stimulate and sustain higher levels of learning and hence levels of learning.

Q19. Describe various interactive media used in teaching and learning.

Ans. Advent of various information and communication technologies facilitate face-to-face interaction among teacher and learner. Satellite-based communication mechanisms have brought new possibilities for interaction directly with experts located at a distance. The degree of interactivity however varies as it depends on the ability of the technology to provide feedback to the source quickly and efficiently. These interactive media for learning can be discussed as follows:

(1) Computer based Interactive Media: Computers have be alternatively viewed as objects of instruction, as aids to instruction, and as productivity tools for teachers and students. Each of these represents a valid perspective to the use of computers, but they carry very different implications for the classroom teacher and student. Computers are also viewed as aids to instruction, providing the curricular support mentioned earlier. Computers may be at the heart of presentation systems for teachers, deliver independent study materials to learners, or provide rich resources for resource-based approaches. Certainly, this is a significant and growing role for computers to play in K-12 education.

A dominant role for computers to play in education is as personal productivity tools for teachers and students. For example, from this perspective, users learn how to use the computer to facilitate research, design and layout reports, perform word processing, design spreadsheets and search electronic bulletin boards. This is a very important role for the computer to play in our schools, especially given the pressures on our schools to prepare computer literate individuals.

(2) Teleconferencing/videoconferencing: Broadcast television is essentially a one-way medium but well designed broadcasts can involve learners and make them active. Teleconferencing or videoconferencing is one of the most interactive media available to replicate the classroom situation at a distance. Being an audio-visual medium, teleconferencing has the inherent advantages of being able to carry both visual and aural messages to the learners. Since television is very useful in portraying demonstrations of skills and processes, it can facilitate visual portrayal of real events, graphics, animation, etc. The visual element of video can engage the mind of the learner and enhance the learning experience by providing rich visuals and cultural context. It can take learners to places/situations which cannot possibly be shown in a classroom. The main limitation of the medium, however, is the cost, which continues to be high. Many a time, there may be less than full exploitation of capabilities and lack of interactivity in many applications because of unfamiliarity with the equipment. If video transmission disappears the session can carry on but if audio link breaks down, the session dust end.

The following steps may be taken for encouraging interactivity through teleconferencing:

(i) **Prepare Participants for the Session in Advance:** Distributing pre-readings or questions to the participants is a good practice. Notifying participants in advance about the session and also about the topics to be taught is also desirable. These can be some of the measures to be taken.

(ii) **Establish Rapport:** The teacher has to get friendly with the learners and help them to overcome inhibitions in using the media for communication. The participants may also be asked to introduce themselves as they speak.

(iii) **Encourage Participation:** It is necessary to present the content but instead of spending too much time on presentation, it is necessary to give the participants opportunity to speak.

For using teleconferencing, its reach and accessibility need to be carefully considered. Moreover, the mindset has to go beyond classroom teaching techniques to effectively harness the visual element of the medium. Hence, power point presentations may be used along with oral communication.

(3) Interactive Radio: Audio is a simple medium and in view of its reach and availability, it is especially useful when used in an interactive mode. Radio is essentially a one-way medium. It has been used in two-way mode by various educational institutions in developing countries of Latin America, Africa, and Asia. The personal and intimate nature of the medium facilitates interaction between teachers/experts located in the studio and the learners in their homes, workplaces etc. They can listen to the presentations of the experts and pose questions with the help of telephones, faxes, etc. The Indira Gandhi National Open University has initiated live radio counseling sessions through various stations of All India Radio and the response has been found to be quite encouraging.

(4) Audio Conferencing and Audio Graphics: Audio conferencing links teachers and learners via a two-way speech channel over telephone lines or sometimes by radio and reaches learners, usually in study centres but also in homes. It is a fully interactive medium in which real time interaction requires learners and teachers to coordinate their schedules. Since audio conferencing takes place in an exclusively audio environment, verbal proficiency and questioning skills of the teacher are crucial for successful teaching and learning. However the problems with the telephone line and equipment breakdowns can limit interactivity.

In audio graphics, special equipments using telephone and graphics technologies during audio conferences allow everyone in the conference to handwrite or type text and draw graphics that are seen in all locations in the conference. It is also a fully interactive medium which facilitates real-time interactivity; however, it requires a proper coordination of schedules.

❑❑❑

Chapter-2

Technology for Education and Training

Q1. How does technology help in learning the skills that require physical interaction with the world, and/or carrying out an experiment?

Ans. Technology has been helping in teaching and learning since its advent. It can be discussed as follows:

(1) Technology facilitate and assists in the authentication, search, identification, storing and processing of the digital material available online.

(2) Motivating learners: Motivation of the learner is the most important factor in learning. Technology helps and facilitates the process of providing motivation during the process of learning. Through technology it is possible to provide immediate feedback to learners. For instance in a multimedia CD, quizzes and other assessment exercises may be included. On attempting these questions learners are provided with immediate feedback.

(3) Collaborative learning: Technology like the Internet provides learners with an access to rich educational resources, their teachers and other experts and even their peers and thus learning becomes collaborative.

(4) Some technologies like the Internet allow learners to utilise more than one sense organ as instructions are provided as multimedia. The content may also be interactive and while shyness or crowded classrooms may inhibit interactions, technology facilitates it in distance learning.

(5) Technology can help in learning subjects like history, and/or future trends because it can reconstruct situations and thus facilitate visualisation of going back and forth in time. A few examples might be: journey through ancient India, a trip to future India, or a devastated or polluted environment, etc.

(6) Technology can be great help to the multilingual population, with automated translators available both to teachers and students.

(7) Simulations possible through technology enables learners to interact in real time with the situations created. Simulation has its own advantages and provides learners with real life experiences. The ideal situation would be for each student to have access to laboratories and scope for field work.

(8) Technology can deploy simulation via micro world, tele-robotic technologies. With these technologies students can interact with the virtual environment created and engage in the physical experiment. In tele-immersive environment for teaching and learning, a three dimensional virtual space, which mimics the real space visually, aurally and tactually, both the student/apprentice and teacher can meet and interact. There would be many advantages of such an environment such as:

(i) The students and teachers do not have to be physically present at the same place as technology can connect them.

(ii) The teacher can teach several students through technology and yet the student would feel that he/she is the only one getting the teacher's full attention.

(iii) Technology would facilitate demonstration/coaching of physical and/or mechanical skills (such as surgery, operating complex machinery, etc.), which requires true spatio-temporal observations of the demonstrator. In turn the tutor can make the same spatiotemporal observations of the students and provide not only verbal but also mechanical feedback. This feedback is critical for the apprentice since it will give him/her a sense of being touch with reality.

(9) It can serve as a tool for the differently challenged population, (this also includes the elderly). Technology can serve as an extension and enhancer for their missing capabilities, which could be perceptual, physical or cognitive so that they can also receive the delivered

information. For example, for the visually impaired, one can have Braille lettered terminals and input/output devices. For paraplegic learners there are several robotic customised devices for interacting with teaching material. For the slow learners, the teaching material can be adapted for ensuring drill practice, exercise, feedback, etc.

(10) Technology allows learning anytime, anywhere and at one's own pace. Technology allows independent learning and facilitates access to data and helps in processing it and sharing results. It thus helps in constructive learning. Storing and retrieving information are also easy.

Q2. Discuss audio-based technologies for education and training.

Ans. Its been decades since we are using audio-based technologies. A number of other audio-based technologies can be used to extend the reach of teachers and it also enhances interaction. Audio based technology has contributed a lot to the upgrading of societal education standards, realizing the strength of this tool of mass communication ,Benjamin Darrow, 1932, founder and first Director of the Ohio School of the Air has said "Radio may come as a vibrant and challenging textbook of the air". This statement is considerably quite correct and even today as we are using this technology for imparting information and education to remote areas. For example, in India, Gyan Vani, a network of FM dedicated radio stations for educational broadcast by IGNOU, under an agreement between IGNOU and Prasar Bharti. These Radio Stations have a reach of nearly 60-75 km around their locations. In addition to broadcast (in one-way) interactive radio counseling (two-way communication) is also conducted from these stations. Besides radio counselling we have following other technologies which can be used for above said purpose:

- **Podcasting:** A podcast is a digital medium consisting of an episodic series of audio, video, radio, PDF, or ePub files subscribed to and downloaded through web syndication or streamed online to a computer or mobile device. Podcasting as an educational technology is a relatively new technology. Initially it was used only for delivering audio programmes, especially music but now, video programmes are also available through it. The term Podcasting is made up of two words – iPod and broadcasting and was initially used to describe the process of creating and publishing a digital radio broadcast over the Internet. Since the last few years, it gained popularity because of its potential for providing multimedia services over the internet and it is today a useful tool for educational purposes. It offers facility for providing multimedia instructions. These facilities are available over the Internet, which with the help of certain technologies for playback can make it available on personal computers. The content being delivered through video casting, are as multimedia computer files that can contain data as audio, images, text, PDF, graphics, animation, etc. Educational content is provided as a file on the Internet, which is available to the user through certain software that can retrieve and process the data thus received.

Podcasts are usually free of charge and therefore can benefit the learners if they have the necessary software besides mobile phones or computers to retrieve the information. Today podcasts are recorded for students and teachers use them for their professional development. Podcasts are prepared even by learners and shared with their teachers and peers by putting it on the Internet. Learning is thus personalized, active a creative experience for students. Submitting assignments, viewing demonstrations, hearing lectures without going to classrooms are possible through this technology.

Podcasts delivered over the Internet support on-demand learning, frees students from the compulsion of attending classes. Similarly, it can be used for training people far away. Educational institutions have started to support podcasting by providing the necessary facilities as severs for producing and exchanges content. Podcasting servers of some reputed companies also allow Podcasts to be attached to blogs (Refer Glossary) as files are attached to e-mails. Educational Podcast network are today being developed to bring together, a repertoire of Podcasts for teachers and learners so that they can explore and access suitable content.

- **Broadcasting:** The word "broadcasting" refers to cast or throw forth something in all directions at the same time. So in that sense, a radio or television broadcast is a program that is transmitted over airwaves for public reception by anyone with a receiver tuned to the right signal channel. It is always a one-way communication.

The term is sometimes used in e-mail or other message distribution for a message sent to all members, rather than specific members, of a group such as a department or enterprise.

On the Internet, certain Web sites deliver original or redistributed broadcasts from existing radio and television stations, using streaming sound or streaming video techniques. For distance education, audiocassettes and audio conferencing are commonly used. New multimedia technologies enable educators to add hypermedia in teaching. When hypermedia audio links added to computer based learning materials, for instance, if clicked on a highlighted area of a content, it will open new link that provide instruction in audio form.

Q3. Discuss web based technologies for educational training purpose.

Ans. As training professionals decide how to transition to the web, they have a host of technologies from which they can choose, beginning with the earliest use of the Internet, to the most technologically advanced capabilities. As with traditional training methods, web-based technologies can be used in conjunction with other methods and media in the delivery of a training program. Each of these potential technologies is described below, in increasing order of technological sophistication.

Asynchronous Text Communication (e-mail, listservs, newsgroups): E-mail, listservs, and newsgroups are examples of asynchronous text communication. In this type of communication, trainers and trainees send and receive messages at different times. For example, a trainee may send a question to the trainer in the morning, and the trainer may respond to the question later in the day. While perhaps the least sophisticated of the Web-based technologies, there are advantages to communicating asynchronously. To begin with, trainers' and trainees' schedules need not be in synch; they can participate in the training program at different times. Asynchronous communication also allows trainees and trainers more time to formulate thoughtful questions, responses, and comments.

Synchronous Text communication (chats): Synchronous text communication, also known as chatting, allows the sending of messages in real time. This technology allows for a discussion to take place at the same time among trainees and trainers connected via the World Wide Web. Since synchronous text communication more closely resembles a classroom discussion, exchanges among trainees are more spontaneous and less controlled.

Web Pages (HTML): Web pages are the cornerstone of the World Wide Web. A Web page typically consists of text and graphics (similar to what might appear on a written page), with a collection of Web pages being called a Website. Through the use of HTML, or HyperText Markup Language, visitors to a Web page can click on specific text or images to gain access to other Web pages and files. As with other computer-based training programs, trainees can progress through the training at their own pace. Hypertext links may also be created to other Web sites external to the training program.

- **Web-Based Media Delivery (video/audio clips):** Web pages can also be designed to deliver video and/or audio clips on a desktop or laptop computer, building upon the features of basic Web pages consisting of text and graphics.
- **Web-Based Interactive Multimedia:** Web-based training can also be delivered as interactive computer-based training (CBT) modules (Fritz, 1997). They may be self-contained CBT programs which have been programmed to run directly through Web pages or as downloaded programs which execute on the trainee's desktop.
- **Web-Based Conferencing (groupware, synchronous video/audio):** Taking the synchronous text communication technology to a higher level, Web-based conferencing allows text as well as other forms of communication to be exchanged among individuals. Groupware supports the sharing of documents and data (e.g., spreadsheets or software programs) so that several individuals in different locations can work with them at the same time. Synchronous audio and video enable individuals to see and hear one another, in a manner similar to audio and video conferencing systems. While this technology requires more computing power and technical support than

other Web-based delivery methods, it most closely simulates trainers and trainees working together in the same classroom.

Q4. Discuss the software which we use in making of self learning material in print technologies.

Ans. Print technology can be considered as the evolution of technology in education. It revolutionised the access to education. It is the print technology which make possible education for everyone in their hand and this mantra of technology has been producing more and more students every year. Classrooms emerged for teachers to disseminate content with the printed text as the mainstay of teaching and learning.

So far the print medium has been the mainstay of providing education. As a result of this the concept of self-learning materials in the print medium evolved. Printing is today different from what it was earlier as various printing technologies evolved in past years. Printed text could be as a book, brochure, newsletter, PowerPoint presentation, poster, etc. Different types of softwares are available to help us in these activities. These are as follows:

(1) Painting and Drawing: Pictures can be either illustrations or photographs. If you want to get graphics into a Web page or multimedia presentation, you either have to create them in some kind of graphics application by drawing or painting them right there in the application, or bringing them into the application via a digital camera or scanner, and then editing and saving them in a form suitable to your medium.

Many software applications offer a variety of features for creating and editing pictures on the computer. Even multimedia authoring and word processing programs include some simple features for drawing on the computer. So, painting and drawing application in computer graphics allows the user to pick and edit any object at any time. The basic difference is as follows:

- Drawing in a software application means using tools that create shapes such as squares, circles, lines or text, which the programme treats as discrete units. If you draw a square in PowerPoint, for example, you can click anywhere on the square and move it around or resize it. A drawing program allows a user to position standard shape (also called symbols, templates, or objects) which can be edited by translation, rotations and scaling operations on these shapes. Example of software facilitating this are Adobe Illustrator, PowerPoint, etc.

- Painting functions do not create shapes. Unlike a drawing function, a paint function changes the colour of individual pixels based on the tools you choose. You need a paint function to create change in colours in the image. Example of such softwares are Adobe Photoshop. paintbrush, KidPix, which offers both drawing and painting for children has a simplified interface and lacks the sophisticated functions a professional artist might want.

(2) Presentation Graphics: These are used for presentation of slides with information in the form the text, charts, graphs etc., to make you presentation effective. To create these, presentation graphics may be used. The softwares used are known as Presentation Graphics softwares. Apple's Keynote, Openoffice's (Star Office-by Sun Microsystems) Impress, Microsoft PowerPoint Macromedia Director (for multimedia presentations, incorporating moving pictures, and sounds) are some of these softwares. They are capable of depicting information in the form of a slide show (A slideshow is a display of a series of chosen images, which is done for artistic or instructional purposes. Slideshows are conducted by a presenter using an apparatus which could be a computer or a projector).

Three major functions of presentation graphics are:

- as an editor that allows text to be inserted and formatted,
- a method for inserting and manipulating graphic images, and
- a slide-show system to display the content.

Custom graphics can also be created in other programmes such as Adobe Photoshop or Adobe Illustrator and then imported. With the growth of video and digital photography, many programmes that handle these types of media also include presentation functions for displaying them in a similar "slide show" format. Similar to programming extensions for an Operating system or web browser, "add ons" or plugins for presentation programmes can be used to enhance their capabilities. For example, it would be useful to export a PowerPoint presentation as a Flash animation or PDF document. This would make delivery through removable media or sharing over the Internet easier. Since PDF files are designed to be shared regardless of platform and most web browsers already have the plugin to view Flash files, these formats would allow presentations to be more widely accessible.

(3) Photo Editing: Photo-editing programmes are paint programmes. They include many sophisticated functions for altering images and for controlling the image, like light and colour balance. For the most part, any paint program can open and display a digital photo image, but it will probably not offer the range and depth of features that a true photo-editing programme like PhotoShop does. Some softwares used for image manipulation are PhotoShop (Adobe), FireWorks (Macro Media. Corel (owned by Corel). Almost everything you see in print or on the web has gone through PhotoShop. With PhotoShop you can make anything look real.

(4) Graphics or Graphical Tricks: This technology has heavily influenced multimedia and has helped in strengthening the print technology by adding text, images, illustrations and colours. Graphics could be of different types like drawings, paintings, photographs, or text represented as charts, graphs, or there could even be pictorial representations. Image Manipulation; Vector Graphics; Page Layout; Website development; Presentation Software; Video Editing; DVD Production; Animation and Interactivity, etc. are some of the software that help us in preparation and presentation of graphics.

(5) Creating print medium: Page layout, presentation, multimedia authoring and Web development programs usually contain a variety of graphics functions ranging from the simple to the complex, but their main purpose is composition. They allow you to create or import text and graphics and, perhaps, sound, animation and video. Most of the graphic features in these types of programs are limited for drawing functions because you will do other kinds of work through other facilities like creating text through word processing, using paint programmes, etc. and then import your work to arrange the different pieces in the composition programs (Some multimedia authoring systems, however, also offer painting and drawing functions). The differences in composition programs are mainly in the form of their output. Page layout programs, such as PageMaker and Quark Express, are for composing printed pages; presentation and multimedia authoring programs, such as PowerPoint and HyperStudio, are for slide shows and computer displays; and Web development applications, like Netscape

Composer, are for Web pages. If you are going to prepare a magazine, newspaper or a book in that case, you need a page layout program. The well known softwares in page layout are: Quark Express, Page Maker (Adobe), Indesign (Adobe), Publisher (Microsoft). To create posters and brochures, designers commonly use vectorised programs. Vectors are useful because the prints are of good quality and you can scale them up to make them large, or scale them down to make them small, and there is not distortion. Example: Adobe Illustrator.

Q5. What is teleconferencing? Write the types of teleconferencing.

Or

What are the advantages and limitations of teleconferencing?

Ans. Teleconferencing can be referred as the interactive electronic transmission method for real-time, two-way conversations among groups of individuals in different geographical locations. In education this communications system is frequently used in courses for students and staff development for teachers called distance learning.

It was first introduced in the 1960s with American Telephone and Telegraph's Picture phone.

Interactive teleconferencing with both audio and visual component are today used for instructional teleconferencing with both audio and visual component are today used for instructional purposes in distance education. It involves interactive group communication among three or more people in two or more locations through an electronic medium.

Today, teleconferencing is used in many ways. There are three basic types:

- Video conferencing- communication as in television with both audio and video .
- Computer conferencing-printed communication (text) through keyboard terminals.
- •Audio-conferencing -verbal communication via the telephone with optional capacity for telewriting or telecopying.

Since Video conferencing is in great demand, we will briefly discuss some of the technical issues related to it.

(1) Audio teleconferencing: The least expensive and oldest form of teleconferencing is audio teleconferencing, sometimes simply referred to as audioconferencing. Auioconferencing is a non-visual communications format in which participants can hear, but not see, each other. To communicate you will need a common dial-up telephone line, speakerphones, and directional microphones. An audioconference can be as simple as a conference-call on a telephone line. In contrast, you might want to connect up to participants who can talk to each other at more than three locations. In this case, you will need a more complicated audioconferencing system. In addition to the basic equipment, you will need to include an audio telephone bridge. This bridge is an electronic system, either provided by a telephone company or owned by a school system, that adjusts the audio volume and connects multiple telephones at participating locations.

(2) Videoconferencing: The most expensive and sophisticated teleconferencing system is video teleconferencing, or simply, videoconferencing. Ideally, full-motion video and audio transmissions are exchanged at various participating sites via a satellite, cable, or microwave network.

More commonly used in education sites today is the one-way television or video and two-way audio videoconferencing system. Besides audio feedback from students by telephone or speakerphone, there is another system in use today. It is sometimes called an electronic non-verbal system, in which students use response keypads to elicit yes-no answers or send more complex alphanumeric messages to the instructor. Regardless of response alternative, the primary reason for selecting the one-way video, two-way audio design is its lower price. In comparison, two-way television and two-way audio is the most desirable videoconferencing system, but the cost of this full video and audio system is beyond most education budgets at the present time.

There are basically two kinds of VTC (Videoteleconference) systems:

(1) Dedicated systems have all required components packaged into a single piece of equipment, usually a console with a high quality remote controlled video camera.

(2) Desktop systems are add-ons (hardware boards, usually) to normal PCs, transforming them into VTC devices. A range of different cameras and microphones can be used with the board, which contains the necessary codec and transmission interfaces. Video conferences carried out via dispersed PCs are also known as e-meetings.

Video conferencing is already done for telecast of news and is now also being done for educational purposes.

Advantages and Disadvantages of Teleconferencing

Advantages: Although economy is a big advantage of teleconferencing, there are several other advantages:

- Learning is collaborative.
- Problems in leaving home/place of work are solved.
- Socialising is much less as compared to a face to face meeting; therefore, meeting are shorter and more focused to the primary purpose of the meeting.

Limitations: While teleconferencing is characterised by many advantages, it also has certain disadvantages:

- There could be difficulty in determining speaking order and duration of speech of the participants and one person may monopolise the session.
- Greater participant preparation and preparation time needed.
- Informal, one-to-one, social interactions are not possible.
- Technical failures with equipment, and connections may spoil the meeting.
- Unsatisfactory for complex interpersonal communication, such as for negotiations. Such meetings may include more of impersonal discussions and hence may not create rapport.
- Lack of familiarity with the equipment, the medium itself, and communication skills, in participants may make the conferencing ineffective.

To minimise some of the potential problems, users should carefully evaluate their meeting needs and objectives. Teachers should also assess their audience. For example, the size of the group, their level of experience with teleconferencing, and the extent of their familiarity with each other may be assessed prior to the session. In spite of all the limitations, teleconferencing represents a unique alternative to the traditional face to face meeting.

Q6. Describe the various features of different technologies used for designing learning materials.

Ans. Developments in technology have modified the face-to-face interaction of traditional classroom teaching to mobile learning and virtual education. Percival, Ellington and Race (1993), identified technology of education as an intangible area which should be stressed on the techniques of teaching and learning instead of hardware and software.

Technology in designing a courseware includes activities like defining the goals and specifying the objectives of the courseware, structuring the content into courses, may be even blocks and units, assigning credits i.e. weight for the various components of the courseware, arranging the components in a logical sequence, selecting and analysing learning experiences to meet the goals and objectives, devising modes of assessment and monitoring, selecting the medium of delivery of instructions, etc. All these activities require access of data, sharing of data and active collaboration among the team of experts designing the courseware. Information and communication technology like computer and internet for data access, saving and sharing the data play an important role at the designing stage.

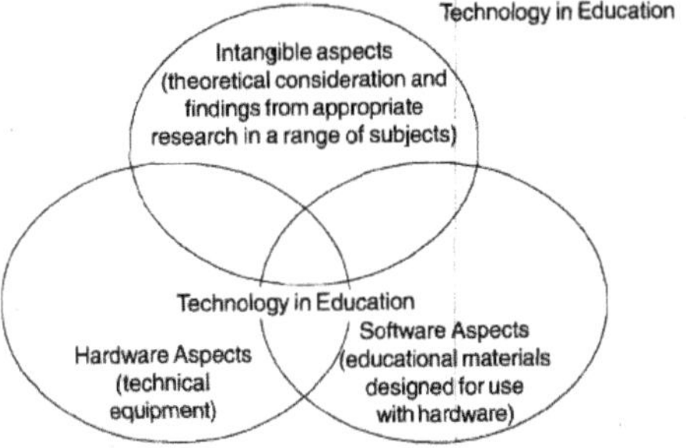

Fig. 2.1: Different aspects of educational technology

When we have many options for a single things than we need to choose based from them. Bates have resolved this problem by listing a range of technologies from low-tech/low-interactivity media to more sophisticated high-tech/high-interactivity packages.

The technological developments according to Bates (2005) are as follows:

- Audio cassettes
- Video cassettes
- Audio conferencing
- Computer based learning
- Audio graphics systems

- Cable TV
- View data/Tele-Text
- Satellite TV
- Laser video-discs
- Video conferencing
- Computer conferencing
- Compact discs
- Internet
- Electronic mail
- World Wide Web
- Digital video discs
- Search engines
- Fibre optics
- Mobile phones
- Learning objects
- Wireless networks
- Portals
- e-Portfolios
- Simulations
- Expert Systems
- Virtual Reality (VR)

The selection and incorporation of technology must be considered during the designing stage itself and it depends on the following parameters:

(1) Collaborative Intellectual Networking: Designing courseware is not the job of a single person but is usually done in teams. Hence, collaboration and networking are essential and technology facilitates these processes. Developers of coursewares are required to develop suitable content which are standard based, focused on outcomes and interactive. These objectives are met by using technology to design, deliver and support the content. Networking, through ICT, facilitates quick exchange of information among the team members. Conferencing over the networks allows the different members of the team to work together even when they are away from each other. Such networking is today made easy by Satellites. Today there are also softwares like email, calendering, chat, etc. designed to help people involved in a common task to achieve their goals.

Courseware designing also has to consider its mode of delivery. How to facilitate interaction between learners and teachers should be considered. Hence whether component with face to face interaction would be included, work shops where resource persons would be there, conferencing facilities would be included and the like, have to be decided at the designing stage itself to clarify the role of technology for delivery later on. Another aspect is that the courseware developed has to allow interaction between the content and the learner and Web-based courses, CDs with content in multimedia, etc. are effective in this regard. The former is especially effective as collaboration among learners with teacher and other experts are made possible. Courseware designers now use technology to design a platform where ideas, experiences and best practices are shared for promoting communication. TAPPED IN and Inquiry Learning Forum are two such teacher-driven and teacher-supported collaborative networks.

(2) Software for Designing Courseware: Planning and designing courseware is teamwork and involves workshops, brain storming and meeting with experts in the area of study. Objectives of the course have to be framed in consonance with the goals of education. How to reduce the isolation of distance learners by making the courseware interactive also has to be planned. Scaffolding features like introduction, glossary, list of suggested reading, etc. have to be planned. The level of the course also has to be decided. Activities and questions that would aid constructive learning are also to be developed. Finally in view of the needs of the learners, the course outline is developed. The presentation of the content also has to be chalked out for each unit of the course. Media selection for delivery of instructions needs to be taken care of at this stage. Theories of learning should guide the entire process of course designing.

Thus course designing is an activity that involves a lot of planning and decision-making and of course teamwork and networking. Hence, it is becoming dependent on technology. Computers are definitely handy for data storing, and processing during designing stage. The Internet is useful for assessing information and sharing it. For instance curriculum of other universities and educational institutions in that area can be accessed. Conferencing facilities especially help people at distant places to work jointly. Networking helps in linking experts, resource persons and the course designers. Several software programmes have been developed for designing coursewares. There are many reputed companies that provide educational institutions of higher learning with online software tools for designing courseware for distance education and training provided by corporate houses and other organisations. Blackboard, Web CT (now owned by Blackboard) are some of the providers of tools for designing courses for online learning. Groupware (programs that help people work jointly while at distance from each other) are especially helpful for this.

(3) Data Access: When designing courseware, adequate attention needs to be paid to its accessibility by learners for whom the courseware is being developed. Technology leading to web sites with relevant content, electronic databases and online educational resources like online libraries, etc, if included, then it has to be ascertained that learners are able to access them. The technology must provide more than just access to the resources. The technology should act like a helping hand to the teacher and also the learner to view, save, analyse and reflect upon the data.

Q7. What do you mean by authoring software? List some of the authoring software.

Ans. Authoring software are applications that aim to reduce the effort needed to produce software, by assuming responsibility for mechanical aspects of the task, by guiding the author, and by offering predefined elements that an author can package together to suit a particular need.

Authoring software provides an integrated environment for binding together the content and functions of your project. Authoring systems typically include the ability to create, edit and import specific types of data; assemble raw data into a playback sequence or cue sheet; and provide a structured method or language for responding to user input.

So these software are used to develop CAL (Computer Aided Learning) packages for making self-learning material. Different kinds of authoring software are available which help in developing applications for general and multimedia platform. These authoring software have been discussed below:

(1) Ezedia: Developed for both the Windows and Macintosh platforms, it helps in creating digital portfolios, storyboards, business presentations, multimedia slide shows, animations and interactive CD-ROM projects.

(2) Hyper Method: Developed for Windows environment, this is suitable for organising distance learning courses by acting as a learning content management system.

(3) Director: It uses movie metaphor for generating applications. Mostly suitable for visual communication applications, it is another product from Macromedia.

(4) Author ware: It is an icon based authoring software developed by Macromedia. In this software one has to drag and drop the objects to generate applications.

(5) Create Together: Developed for Windows environment, it helps in creating animated games, randomly generated puzzles, interactive simulations, searchable multimedia databases, and hyperlinked presenations.

(6) Cyber Editor: Developed for students to enable them to create multimedia documents.

(7) Virtual Cinema: Developed for both the Windows and Macintosh platforms, it is an object-oriented authoring, media integration and delivery/playback tool which can be used with applications involving streaming media.

(8) Question Mark: One of the most widely used authoring software for designing and developing computerised tests and examinations for educational institutions. It can be used over Web based, Windows and Macintosh platforms.

(9) Movie Works: Developed for both the Windows and Macintosh platforms, it is suitable for creating multimedia applications by integrating video, sound, animation, paint and image editing tools. This tool handles quite effectively different formats like analog or digital video, buttons, photos, graphics, animations, 3D, narration, MIDI, MP3, CD music, etc.

(10) Icon Author: Developed Asymetrix, it helps in creating visual layout applications through flowcharts.

(11) Top Class: Developed by WBT systems, this is one of the most popular authoring software.

(12) On Viz.: Developed for Macintosh platforms, it helps in applications for computer-based training, e-learning, electronic books, electronic reference manuals, expert systems, demos, advertising, presentations, simulations, kiosks, games, etc.

(13) mTropolis: used for designing simple multimedia games.

(14) iShell: Developed for both the Windows and Macintosh platforms, it is suitable for creating custom Internet applications, advanced CD-ROM-Internet hybrids and Internet kiosks.

(15) GLpro: It is a multimedia programming language to develop applications for Windows and DOS environments. It is used by Microsoft, Compaq, Intel, etc.

Q8. What do you understand by "desktop publishing? Describe the steps in "desktop publishing"?

Ans. Desktop publishing allows us to create brochures, fliers, newsletters, advertisements, and manuals without having to visit a print shop. Many administrative assistants use desktop publishing software to create high-quality publications that can be printed one at a time in the office or taken to a local print shop for mass duplication. Many desktop publishing programs have predefined templates that allow to add our own text and graphics to quickly customise a publication. You can create your own letterhead, business cards, and business forms with the help of desktop publishing.

While it is similar to word processing in theory, desktop publishing focuses on the layout of text and graphics on a page. Some sophisticated word-processing programs, such as Microsoft Word, can be used for desktop publishing. However, there are other more specialised tools available for creating graphics, adding special effects, and laying out multi-page brochures.

In addition to desktop publishing software, you need an office computer system complete with a keyboard, monitor, and mouse. Optional desktop publishing hardware includes a graphics tablet, a color printer, a scanner, and a digital camera.

Most desktop publishing software programs share certain common tools. They allow you to arrange and format text and graphics

These are as follows:

(1) Computer Graphics: In desktop publishing, the text is processed and manipulated by changing its font, size, color etc. It is represented mainly by characters, words, sentences, paragraphs etc. It should be noticed that sometimes the text is represented in the form of graphics or pictures of text. There are different types of graphics. These may be in the form of pictures. They are used in the form of objects, places, cartoons etc and are used to enhance the visual communication of the text or the message. A graphics can be in the form of an icon, a graph, bullet, border around a piece of text etc. You must have seen graphics in the form of textured background (as used in brochures or on web sites) like in the form of some secenery, geometrical pattern etc. The different forms of graphics are Balloon; Box, Border, Frame; Chart, Graph; ClipArt; Symbols, Signs, Icons.

Different forms of graphics types are as follows:

(i) **Balloon:** These are also known as thought bubbles and are frequently used in comic books.

(ii) **Box, Border, Frame:** These are decorative frames used to highlight a portion of text or image.

(iii) **Chart, Graph:** This is a symbolic representation of data, used to enhance the visual communication of the message.

(iv) **Clip Art:** These are non-photographic graphic images, for example those built-in in Microsoft Word etc.

(v) **Symbols, Signs, Icons:** These are simple representations of ideas and actions.

(2) Graphic Formats: An understanding of graphics format is essential towards the learning of computer graphics. In computer graphics, the coded information is processed by the computer (in the form of bits and bytes) so that a graphic image is displayed in desired manner. The following two types of graphics are discussed briefly:

(i) **BITMAP graphic:** It is composed of pixels. These can be created by MS-Paint or by using some photo-editing software (like Photoshop). One problem with bitmaps is that resizing the bitmaps affects the resolution and the image may be distorted. Common formats for Bitmap images are JPG, GIF, PICT, BMP, TIFF.

(ii) **VECTOR graphic:** It uses geometrical shapes like ponts, lines, curves, etc. that are all based upon mathematical equations. There is maintenance of quality even when the size is manipulated. These can be created by using softwares like CorelDRAW, Illustrator or Freehand etc. Common Vector formats are WMF, EPS, CDR etc. WMF (Windows Metafile Format), although a vector image format, it can combine both vector and raster images.

While desktop publishing is essentially the process of composing text and graphics with the help of computers to make page layouts to produce documents (for example books, newsletters, brochures, etc.), computer graphics is an approach and process behind enhancing visual communication of text and graphics like in the design of logos, graphics, posters, signs or newsletters etc.

Steps in desktop publishing are as follows:

(1) Make basic design decisions.

(2) Make basic text decisions.

(3) Make basic graphics decisions.

(4) Sketch each page on paper as an aid to visual decisions.

(5) Prepare text to be inserted into the desktop publishing document (proofread, use spell check and grammar check).

(6) Prepare styles for text and captions. Use the Word Organizer to copy style-or-create your own.

(7) Prepare graphics elements.

(8) Use Word to create a new document.

(9) Use page setup to set appropriate paper size, margins, and page orientation.

(10) Display the Drawing toolbar.

(11) Use Print Layout view.

(12) Turn on the Drawing Grid (customize it, if needed).

(13) Add the document text prepared in step #5 above. Insert standard text first then add text boxes, frames, and tables.

(14) Place graphics. Place all objects on one page at a time. Convert inline graphics to floating graphics where necessary. Embedded objects are usually left at inline graphics. Set wrapping options and edit wrap points where necessary.

(15) Add front matter and back matter.

(16) Use print preview and test printouts to check the alignment of everything.

(17) Updated any linked objects.

(18) Print the document.

Q9. Explain how technology can be used in the delivery of learning materials.

Ans. Technology-enhanced learning is not a new concept. Educators have integrated technology into their instruction for as long as there have been classrooms. Whether it be through textbooks made possible through the invention of the printing press, an overhead projector, a film strip, or an online simulation, teachers have always looked toward technology to provide students with higher quality learning experiences.

However, innovations in content delivery, assessment methods, and adaptive learning are changing what it means to educate students in the 21st century. New technologies are enhancing our understanding of how students learn and providing instructors the ability to customize course materials and create personalized learning experiences tailored to students' individual needs.

As technology and instructional methods evolve, so do students' expectations for a technology-driven learning experience. Emerging online learning models encourage students to be more active participants in their own learning - allowing them to not just be content consumers, but content creators as well. As digital natives, students want to attend a university that effectively integrates the latest technologies and teaching methods into their education.

There are different type of learning materials, so is the types of delivery. For explaining these in a better way, they can be discussed as follows:

(1) Interactive Multimedia: Interactive multimedia stands for the type of that media which gives the user some navigational controls i.e., Internet.

It allows two-way interaction with multimedia course material, another computer, or another user with direct response to the input, as opposed to one-way communication from TV, video, and other non-responsive media. Interactive attributes commonly include data or text entry, mouse input, touch screens, voice commands, video capture, and real-time interaction. Interactive multimedia can also be interpreted as large subset of educational technology, in particular CBT and CBL. It is reported by Geisman (1988) - that students remember 20% of what they see, 40% of what they both see and hear, and 70% of what they see, hear and do. It has educational effectiveness as there is simultaneous engaging of several senses of the learner. Concerning the additive and potentially synergic advantages of multimedia for learning, the educational value of plain text can be enhanced through multimedia to facilitate comprehension.

(2) Audio and video materials:

(i) **Audio and Video Materials:** These materials mainly comprise audio cassettes, audio disc, broadcast through educational radio, community radio and FM radio; video cassettes, video disc, telecast through national telecast network and cable network. Special equipments are necessary to utilise these Audio and Video Materials supplemented by a good public address system to optimise the reach in the classroom. While using the Audio and Video Materials, the teacher should be able to operate the equipment and in times of failure, should be able to fill the gap.

(ii) **Audio-blogging:** This is a new concept and often referred to as "free downloads". One can use audio files uploaded to a blog, website, hyperlinked from a power point slide, or in your email, podcast, or simply keep them on your computer desktop or on CD, or DVD, to use at any time or any place. When used judiciously, audio can be extremely interactive and motivating to the student.

Audio files can be uniquely useful and effective in online as well as in conventional education. However, Audio files are yet to be used commonly in online education. Teachers tend to merely upload their lecture notes or the printed version to the course website – and audio is not effective for delivering mere pages of the textbook. The file size of even one minute tends to be quite large. Students may find that they need time to adjust to comprehend though they can re-play as often as they need. In addition, the students faraway may not have the bandwidth infrastructure and playback software.

(3) Digital Delivery: Digital delivery allows the learners to immediately receive the product i.e., the item related to process of learning upon completion of payment for that particular item. Digital delivery is ensured by:

(i) **Auto Attachments:** At the end of an order, the institution providing the services can attach the product to the learner confirmation e-mail. By specifying the location of the file on a product by product basis, multiple deliveries can be made for an order by a single learner.

(ii) **Auto Generation of Download Links:** At the end of an order, the institution providing the services can display the hyperlinks to the products. These hyperlinks allow the learner to get more information.

The institution providing the services allows the learners to specify the types of payments that are authorised to use the facilities. This prevents hackers from entering into bogus payments. The institution can decide which payment methods are secure enough to allow auto delivery. Attachments, download links and non-digital products can be intermixed in the same order.

Q10. Describe the delivery and use of technology in the context of special education.

Ans. Some learners needed special education because of their specific behavioral, intellectual, communicational, learning or physical characteristics.

Due to the increasing concern for the differently able individuals technology in Special Education is gaining momentum. It aims to provide equal opportunities in education. One must take into consideration the following factors while identifying the technology for people with special needs.

(1) Strengths in areas such as cognitive processing and communication (e.g., expressive language-speaking)

(2) Previously acquired skills (e.g., aesthetic skills, organisational skills, time-management skills)

(3) Personal characteristics that sustain learning (e.g., self-motivation, willingness to work with others)

(4) Learning preferences (e.g., visual, auditory, kinesthetic or learns best on his or her own or working with others)

(5) Interests and hobbies

(6) Co-curricular activities and achievements

Assistive Technology: While we are trying to impart special education for differently able learners but traditional education or instructional technology also can be used for providing support for special needs children, there is a more specialised or customised technology which is beneficial to the students with some form of disability. This is known as assistive technology.

Assistive technology comprises various devices, media and services put to the service for students with physical, sensory, cognitive, speech, learning or behavioural disabilities. These are used to enhance learning among students and helps them to perform activities which otherwise would be difficult for them to do independently. These range from simple to complex activities like in the form of a pencil grip assisting in writing to touch screen systems. These have applications in activities like reading, vision, writing, hearing, etc. The devices or services for assistive technology for learning may range from low tech to high tech, based on the need. Even a single student may use different technologies to accomplish the learning goals. For example, visually impaired students may take advantage of a Braille keyboard and screen reading software, as well as a talking calculator and talking word processor. The devices or services for assistive technology for learning are given in Table.

Table: Devices of Assistive Technology for Learning

Low-tech	Mid-tech	High-tech
• Raised line paper • Alternative writing surfaces (e.g., white boards) • Alternative writing implements (e.g., magnetic letters, alphabet stamps, magnetic words) • Materials to support memory, focus and organisation (e.g., sticky notes, highlighters, webs)	• Tape recorders • Calculators • Talking calculators • Talking spell checkers • Audio books • Dedicated word processors • Simple voice playback devices (e.g., talking picture frames)	• Specialised software such as: ➢ Talking word processors ➢ Word prediction software ➢ Screen reading software ➢ Scan-and-read software • Dedicated communication devices • Specialised computer access

		such as: ➢ Touch screens ➢ Alternative keyboards ➢ Switch adapted mice ➢ Refreshable Braille display

The tools of assistive technology range from simple to complex and serve different kinds of cognitive, physical or behavioural disability. Some of the tools which are used by children with special needs are mentioned below:

(1) Mathematics:

- Abacus, math line.
- Calculator/calculator with printout.
- Talking calculator.
- Onscreen calculator.
- Software with cueing for math computations.
- Tactile/voice output measuring devices.
- Software that provides onscreen manipulation.
- Math processing software.

(2) Vision

- Eyeglasses.
- Magnifier.
- Large print books.
- Closed circuit television.
- Screen magnification software.
- Screen colour contrast .
- Screen reader, text reader.
- Braille materials.
- Braille translation software.
- Enlarged or Braille/tactile labels for keyboard.
- Alternate keyboard with enlarged keys.
- Braille keyboard and note taker.
- Refreshable Braille computer display.

(3) Hearing

- Pen and paper.
- Computer/portable word processor.
- Signaling device.
- Closed captioning.
- Real-time captioning.
- Computer-aided note taking.
- Flash alert signal on computer.
- Personal amplification system/hearing aid.
- Personal FM system.
- Sound-field FM.

(4) Reading

- Changes in text size/space/colour/background colour.
- Book adapted for page turning (e.g., with page fluffers, three-ring binder and folders).
- Use of pictures with text.
- Talking electronic devices for single words.
- Scanner and talking word processor.
- Electronic books.

(5) Spelling and Writing

- Word cards, word book, word wall.
- Pocket dictionary, thesaurus.
- Electronic dictionary/spell checker.
- Word processor with spell check and grammar check.
- Talking word processor.
- Software with talking spell checker.
- Word prediction software to facilitate spelling and sentence construction .
- Multimedia software for production of ideas.
- Voice recognition software.

(6) Organising and Studying

- Print or picture schedules.

- Low-tech aids to find materials (e.g., colour tabs, coloured paper or folders).
- Highlight text (e.g., markers, highlight tape, ruler).
- Voice output reminders for tasks, assignments, steps to tasks.
- Software for manipulation of objects/concept development. may use alternate access method such as touchscreen.
- Software for organising ideas and studying.
- Hand-held devices with scheduling software.

(7) Printing and Handwriting

- Variety of pencils and pens.
- Pencils with adaptive grips.
- Adapted paper (e.g., raised lines or highlighted lines).
- Slant board.
- Prewritten words or phrases.
- Templates.
- Portable word processor.
- Computer with word processor.

(8) Alternative Computer Access

- Keyboard with accessibility options.
- Keyguard.
- Alternative keyboard.
- Dowel, mouth stick, headpointer with keyboard.
- Word prediction, abbreviation/expansion to reduce keystrokes.
- Alternative mouse (e.g., touchscreen, trackball, trackpad, joystick).
- Onscreen keyboard.
- Switch with Morse code.
- Switch with scanning.
- Voice recognition.

(9) Communication

- Communication board with pictures/words/objects.
- Eye gaze frame.
- Simple voice output device.

- Voice output device with sequencing.
- Voice output display with multimessage capability.
- Voice output device with speech synthesis.

Q11. What do you mean by self-learning Material (SLM)? Discuss the technology used for SLM.

Ans. Self learning, also called autodidacticism, refers to educating oneself. It can be possessed or assessed by reading, listening, observing or even performing but it. Teaching is definitely required but it is not necessary that a human teacher has to be present. The teacher is in-built within the SLM to facilitate learning. Technology definitely helps in self learning as it can deliver the software i.e. the learning material anywhere, anytime and facilitate access to different sources of information necessary to complement/supplement the SLM.

Any learning material that promotes learning through one's own efforts, in the absence of a teacher is SLM. It can be in print medium as well as in other media such as a multimedia CD containing SLM. Or even the adult education programmes broadcast through radio or television can facilitate self learning as they promote learning without the physical presence of a teacher. Modern technologies are greatly facilitating self learning by providing the learners with instant access to information and scope for interacting with the source and sharing information.

Various type of technological resources which are used as SLM have been discussed below:

(1) Audio resources: Audio resources as self-learning materials make the learning situations as real as possible and give us firsthand knowledge through the organs of hearing. Therefore, any device which can be used to make learning experience more concrete and effective, more realistic and dynamic can be considered as SLM.

Today institutions like Central Institute of Educational Technology (CIET, NCERT) and Indira Gandhi National Open University (IGNOU) broadcast radio programmes on a regular basis. Radio programmes can be live or can be recorded. IGNOU regularly provides interactive radio counseling programmes for its students wherein the learners can call through the toll free numbers provided to them and contact the teacher. The shortcoming of a radio i.e. one way communication has been overcome by such programmes. Instructions may also be provided through audio cassettes with recorded lectures/discussions by experts

Recorded audio cassettes provide only one way communication but the advantage is that the programme can be stopped, replayed and one can fast forward to skip a part of the content or rewind it. Thus delivery of instructions is according to the pace of the learners.

(2) Television: Television is one of the effective audio visual tools as it blends sound and pictures, as well as it combines immediacy with remoteness and gives a personal touch to mass communication. Television came to India in 1950. In the beginning years, television transmission was introduced around in Delhi only. And it was expanded to other areas during 1970s and 1980s. Television is a versatile medium of transmitting education through different programmes. It is an exciting means of communication. Useful instructional programmes are being telecasted regularly for the student community on television. A teacher should utilise the TV programmes and make them the basis for discussions on relevant occasions. Television focuses the attention of students of a particular topic. Through television, a good teacher can reach the students spread over distant school, simultaneously and effectively.

(3) Interactive videos: In distance education interactive video refers to two way video conferencing whereby people at both ends can hear and see each other. But in this section we shall discuss about interactive videos that contain educational content in multimedia format. The user can interact with the content. Not all interactive videos require the use of a computer. There may be only a video player, which may allow random access to video segments, a video monitor or TV, and a means of user selection which is usually a hand-held remote control device or bar code reader. These simpler forms do not allow much interactively. As against them there are more advanced ones that require the use of a computer. They allow higher degrees of interactivity.

Interactive movies are also available. Nowadays in some museums, railway stations and other places videos with 'touch screen' are available. One has to merely place a finger on the desired point, say a gallery of old coins, to get information about it. Interactive videos can also be online. Besides entertainment, this technology can also provided education. Laboratory experiments can be performed virtually through interactive videos. A learner may go on a virtual trip to a museum and view a piece of art from various angles.

(i) **Slow play:** It allows the user (learner) to play the video at a slower speed (up to real-time either forward or backward) to understand a process better.

(ii) **Nonlinear or Random access:** Access to the video need not to be from the very beginning. Any segment or frame of the video can be selected and watched. Besides the frame chosen can be watched for any duration.

(4) Conferencing: Conferencing through technology has been found to be useful in the field of education and especially in distance education. As in a real classroom, in a virtual one too a teacher and the learners can engage in interactive learning sessions through technology aided conferencing. This is more economical than participants undertaking travel and staying at the place of conference. Today there are conferences calling services that arrange such conferencing and even provide certain number of toll free calls. The services are available for both on demand conferencing as well as for those scheduled, in advance.

(5) Internet: There are many advantages of web based learning and especially the scope for individualised learning at a convenient place and pace along with scope for interactivity make it attractive to learners. The educational content may be offered as plain text or as multimedia and there may also be included facilities for simulated learning and accessing huge volumes of information through hyperlinks. Web based learning is usually through the information already available online but virtual educational institutions provide customised content and information through synchronous modes like circulars, notices, etc. that are posted to reach all the learners simultaneously and also through asynchronous communication modes such as email and discussion forums to reach out to different learners at different times. Learners can interact by sending online queries and expressing the problems faced in learning. Teachers today are using blogs to post problems while learners are encouraged to post their solutions for them. Discussion groups are being created for the exchange of views and news on a topic among the members. There is thus scope for constructive learning by processing the information, enriching it through hyperlinks and working upon the tasks assigned. There is also provision for monitoring learning through techniques available to check the content (pages) visited by the learner, the frequency of such visits, assignments and portfolios submitted, performance at the tests administered, etc.

(6) Instant messaging: This facility allows real time communication over the Internet and thus facilitates online collaborative learning. Most of these services provide the user with the information about the online availability of people in his/her contact list. This makes it more convenient than an e-mail as a tool for imparting instructions to learners. Instant messaging allows video-conferencing, group web surfing and use of white boards for common use. There is also the facility to record the conversations for future use. Peer-to-peer (P2P) file sharing that facilitates sharing of information by dispersed groups as designated files in each others computers and Instant Messaging (IM) are commonly used groupwares today. Multimedia Messaging Service (MMS), allows the exchange of multimedia messages created by the users themselves and unlike an SMS, with limited capacity for holding message they can hold much more up to several kilo bytes. Further value addition is possible through modern features that allow inbox facility to store huge amounts of information (messages) and this is thus a value addition to the utility of this technology as a tool for education. This facility is used for sending learning materials and connecting to learners.

(7) Podcasting: Educational content delivered through videocasting as multimedia computer files on the Internet can contain data in different forms like audio, images, text, etc. Learners can economically access iPods thus delivered on personal computers with the help of certain technologies for playback. They can in turn interact with their teachers and peers by preparing and posting files containing assignments and other work done. Learning through this technology frees the learners from the need for physical presence in the classrooms. There are educational institutions that support podcasting by providing facilities like servers for exchanging content and also for podcasting attachment of podcasts to blogs.

Q12. Discuss the concept of instructional designing.

Ans. The concept of instructional design suitable for self learning emerged with the popularity of distance learning for the masses. We know that a teacher prepares a lesson plan for teaching in the classroom. S/he plans the objectives and the inputs needed to achieve them. Thus s/he designs the instructional process. Similarly it is important to systematically plan the learning materials and design it when it is delivered through technology. It intends to bring about self learning with the teacher remaining inbuilt within the learning material. Hence, the material has to be designed to provide not only knowledge but also ensure that it is pedagogically sound. It is based upon the behaviouristic and cognitive theories of learning.

Instructional methods can be defined as the procedures selected by trainers and instructional designers to help facilitate learning. To understand the various options for delivering a course or a segment of a course via Web-based training, it is important to first understand how learning is currently facilitated in a corporate setting. Described below are eight instructional methods often used in corporate training today.

- **Case Studies:** A case study is a narrative description of a situation in which learners are asked to identify or solve a problem. While the case study may describe either a real or hypothetical situation, it must be pertinent to the learning experience (Rothwell & Kazanas, 1992).
- **Demonstrations:** In a demonstration, the instructor shows the trainee how a task is performed through actual performance. Some examples of how demonstrations are used include teaching procedures, illustrating principles (why something works), teaching equipment operation (how something works), and setting standards for workmanship (Tracey,1984)
- **Discussions/Debates:** Discussion involves the exchange of ideas and feelings among learners and/or the instructor. Discussions can be used with small or large groups and at various stages of the instructional process (Heinich, Molenda, Russell, & Smaldino, 1996).

  Discussions are a popular method among corporate trainers, since adult learners particularly enjoy sharing personal experiences. Debates, a subset of discussions, force learners to select a position on an issue and develop an argument to defend that position.
- **Games:** In a game, the learners follow a prescribed set of rules to try to attain a challenging goal. A game may involve one learner or a group of learners in the experience (Heinich et al., 1996).

- **Presentations:** In a presentation, the instructor presents facts, concepts, and principles; explores a problem; or explains relationships. This method is used primarily to transfer information from the trainer to the trainees, who participate in a presentation mainly as listeners (Tracey, 1984).
- **Role plays:** A role play is a dramatic representation of a real situation that provides learners the opportunity to practice situations they face or will face on the job (Rothwell & Kazanas, 1992). This method is often used in instructor-led training to provide trainees with the opportunity to practice interacting with others.
- **Simulations:** Simulations place the learner in a scaled down version of a real-life situation. They allow the learner to practice in a safe environment without the expense or risks that would be incurred in real life (Heinich et al., 1996). Simulation can be computer-based or classroom-based.
- **Tutorials:** A tutorial can be in the form of a computer-based lesson, printed instructional materials, or a personal tutor (Heinich et al., 1996). Tutorials are designed to present the learner with new information and guide the learner through the use of the information. A typical flow in a tutorial lesson includes information presentation, question and response, judgment of response, feedback or remediation, and closing (Alessi & Trollip, 1991).

Q13. What role ICT is playing in the context of education? Discuss.

Ans. Information and Communication Technologies (ICT) constitute a topic of growing importance for public policies, notably in the field of education. The integration of ICT in our everyday life transforms our relationship to information and knowledge. It also modifies citizens' engagement with public services and the interaction between schools and learners. The opportunities offered by the use of technology in education are many. It transforms the pedagogy and can lead to an improved and more engaging learning experience. These effects are not limited to the classroom, for example, the transformation of distance education into e-learning and blended learning offers new options for delivery and new opportunities for in-service teacher training and support. The capacity of ICT to build borderless networks represents possibilities for innovative peer learning across territories and countries. In addition to redefining access to knowledge and instructional design and provision, the penetration of ICT in all dimensions of economic, social and cultural activities has far-reaching implications in terms of the skills required to become an active member of society. The ability of students to utilize ICT has become a new requirement for effective education systems. Beyond education, ICT can also represent a new source of economic growth and a powerful tool for social transformation. Hence, through their economic and social effects, ICT contribute to creating a knowledge society and economy. In this context, a major concern for policy-making relates to the modalities for designing and implementing plans and strategies likely to produce such results. This publication aims at addressing precisely this question by illustrating, on the basis of case studies analysis, the importance of having clear policy goals, and of their translation into appropriate strategies and plans. The country experiences reviewed in this publication suggest that effective ICT in education policies depend on three main pillars, namely: access to ICT infrastructures and equipment; teacher capacities; and monitoring. Access to equipment, networks and quality resources is a prerequisite for the deployment and utilization of ICT. Therefore, the integration of technologies in the education system requires a supportive environment. This underlines the importance of policy consistency and the need to take advantage of a broader movement of ICT infrastructure development. In many countries, this also implies forging innovative alliances between the public sector and private companies, which often control the ICT sector. In that respect ICT in education, policies offer a rich example of the potential for public-private partnerships.

Once the technological infrastructure is in place, a major challenge relates to the capacity of teachers to take advantage of the tools and new teaching opportunities offered by ICT. This involves developing teachers' professional capacities but also to establish adequate support mechanisms. Furthermore, beyond technical competencies and coaching, effective utilization of technologies in the classroom ultimately depends on the motivation of teachers.

The major challenge always remains to transform teacher training into improved teacher practices in the classroom. The best incentives for teachers come from the evidence of improved and more efficient teaching practices. Yet, addressing this challenge often involves a cultural change for teachers, which cannot always happen rapidly. The introduction of technologies into the education system on a large scale involves setting up mechanisms and tools to monitor implementation processes and outcomes. In particular, it is essential to develop approaches and indicators to monitor how ICT investments and policies affect teaching practices and students' abilities and knowledge.

Education policy-makers see the dissemination and use of information and communications technologies (ICT) in schools should have as a significant opportunity. They are attracted to the prospect that ICT can improve student achievement, improve access to schooling, increase efficiencies and reduce costs, enhance students' ability to learn and promote their lifelong learning, and prepare them for a globally competitive workforce. As the power and capability of computers have increased, as they have become interconnected in a worldwide web of information and resources, as they provide a conduit for participation and interaction with other people, as they have become linked to other devices, and as their costs have come down.

Q14. Discuss technology for the purpose of training in education.

Ans. Today different types of technologies are available to support an enhance learning and are used for imparting training. Technologies like video, audio, digital movie making, podcasting, laptop computing, mobile and handheld technologies, etc. are being commonly used for training and teaching. It is very important for us to select the right kind of technologies and understand the fact that different technologies serve different purposes in the education system. For instance, email, chat and blogging promotes the education network of students, teachers and trainers, which besides facilitating exchange of information, improves communication skills. Word processing, presentation and spreadsheet promote productivity and organisational skills. Simulations and modeling software promotes the understanding of concepts in reality. Hence, it is essential to consider how these technologies differ and what features make them important as tools for education. There are following types of technologies used for the purpose of training in education:

(1) Hardware Technologies:

(i) Computer: In the last decade or so, the hardware technology of the computer has undergone many changes. From few kilobytes of RAM (Random Access Memory), now the PCs have huge storage space. Other drives and monitors have also emerged with better performance and lower cost. These fast changes ensure unlimited possibilities of using video, audio and simulations in teaching and training.

(ii) Mobile and handheld Devices: Mobile/handheld devices such as iPod, PDAs, (personal digital assistants) and mobile devices are widely used in education both as academic and administrative tools. Following are some of the possible ways to use mobile/handheld devices in teaching/training:

(a) Different activities like interviews, oral examination, oral report, presentation, group discussion, etc. can be recorded for future use, for tutor evaluation, peer evaluation, and self-evaluation.

(b) Learners can listen to authentic audio materials e.g. music, speech, interview audio book, poem, etc. at their own timings.

(c) Learners can create and access multimedia materials e.g. movie, documentary, visual glossary, presentation, assignments, projects, etc.

Computers can be very useful for storing huge amount of data related to training such as trainee profile, results of evaluation, etc. This is stored in the hard drive of the computer.

The terms 'hard drive' and 'hard disk' are used interchangeable. Today's hard disks provide fast access and can hold several gigabytes of information as compared to megabytes on floppy disks. But the hard disk is permanently fixed in the computer cabinet; We rarely plug it out because detaching it frequently is not safe. Hence, to carry data we need some removable memory disks that are described below:

(i) CD-ROMS: Compact disks can store approximately 650-800 MB of data or 74-80 minutes of music. Most software programs today are shipped on CD-ROMs instead of floppy disks. All computers today come with CD-ROM drives that are part of the computer's multimedia configuration. They are connected to a sound card, which provides the computer with stereo speaker capabilities, which you may have used for musical CD-ROMs to be played on your computer. These drives are read only and cannot be used for recording data.

(ii) USB/Flash Drive: USB drives are one of the popular removable disks in current time. It is a plug-and-play portable storage device that uses flash memory and is lightweight enough to attach to a key chain. These drives can be used in place of a floppy disk, Zip drive disk, or CD. When the user plugs the device into their USB port, the computer's operating system recognises the device as a removable drive. Unlike most removable drives, a USB drive does not require rebooting after it is attached. It also does not require batteries or an external power supply, and is not platform dependent. Several USB drive manufacturers offer additional features such as password protection, and downloadable drivers that allow the USB drive to be compatible with older systems that do not have USB ports. USB drives are available in capacities ranging from 32 MB to 8 gigabytes, depending on the manufacturer, in a corresponding range of prices.

(2) Software Technologies: In contrast to the hardware, software are the non-physical components of the computer system like concept, idea or procedure, generally a set of instruction called programs and a set of programs which give a finite output. These software tools include those for word processing, spreadsheets, graphics, communications tools, multimedia, simulation, etc. There are following various types of software tools we use:

(i) Presentation Tools: In today's world, it is very important for us to present our ideas effectively; one way is the use of graphical presentation tools. We have different presentation tools available and among these, a popular one is Microsoft's Power Point presentation tools which is a part of Microsoft Office like Microsoft Word. It allows the presenter to create high quality presentations. It is provided with options for consistency in design and colour. Different PowrPoint templates are available with thousands of color schemes available and a complete set of easy-to-use tools assures you have everything you need to get your point across and share information with others. A PowerPoint presentation is a collection of your slides, handouts, speaker's notes, and your outline, all in one presentation file.

(ii) **Word Processing Tools:** Word processing is an ability to create, store, and print documents using a computer program called a word processor which provides special capabilities beyond that of a text editor such as the WordPad program that comes as part of Microsoft's Windows operating systems. Their basic functions include typing, saving documents, and opening documents, copying, printing and checking spelling. As mentioned above there are many different names of software for different operating systems like Microsoft Word, Word Perfect, WordPad, AppleWorks, etc.

(iii) **Multimedia Tools:** Multimedia is the term for different media like text, graphics, animation, sound, and video all wrapped in one interactive package. The basic idea is to manage and co-ordinate the various devices of communication and entertainment electronics with the computer. Multimedia tools can help us in creating presentations, games, animations, which further promote the interactive ways of learning. Multimedia has emerged as an effective way for students to develop projects that incorporate text, graphics, sound, and video. You can use Microsoft PowerPoint as a multimedia tool to create presentations, multimedia projects, etc. Some multimedia tools for primary class students are also available like Kid Pix Studio and JumpStart, which provide tools for students to paint pictures as well as add text, animation, video, sound effects, and music to create an exciting multimedia project. Some tools are available for trainees interested in creating, manipulating, and editing visuals such as photographs as for e.g. Adobe's Photoshop. Some tools are also available for audio and video production such as imovie, practica Musica, songworks, and kidMusic.

(iv) **Graphical Tools:** A picture can communicate a message that sometimes a thousand words cannot do because we live in a visual world; and the human mind can comprehend and retain concepts learnt through visual description for longer time.

That's why using graphics in teaching can play a very important role. Paint brush which is available with Windows Operating System is one of the graphical tools. However some more graphical tools are available which provide better options, better graphical user interface, libraries, etc. to design better graphics such as Adobe Systems Incorporated, Corel Corporation, Live Picture and Macromedia Incorporated. However, there are several sites on the Web that can assist the creation of graphics. You may try some online free services like Gif Wizard, Map Maker, Pixel site, etc.

(v) **Data Analysis Tools:** Electronic databases and spreadsheets are popular computer tools for teachers and for students/trainees. Students/trainees need skills in locating, evaluating, analysing, classifying, comparing, calculating, and drawing conclusions based on a set of information. Teachers/students at the beginning level may use them for classification of data, at the next level for comparing and contrasting trends, at the expert level, they can use what-if feature and carry out activities like plotting graph for trigonometry questions. Some popular spreadsheet products are File maker and MS-Excel, and database products are MS-Access, Oracle, and DB2, etc.

(vi) **Simulation:** The idea behind using simulations as pedagogical tools relies on the idea that experience is the best teacher. Use of simulations include animated narrative vignettes (ANV). ANVs are cartoon-like video narratives of hypothetical and reality- based stories involving classroom teaching and learning. In one way or another simulations of real-time environments have been used as a tool for teaching and training in many areas and disciplines. This has been the case especially in areas like medicine or in training soldiers, where practice in real-time environments involves risks and high costs. Simulations for training typically come in one of three categories, the first one is Live-Simulation in which real people use simulated equipment in the real world. Next is Virtual-Simulation where real people use simulated equipment in a simulated world or "virtual environment", and last one is

Constructive-Simulation in which case simulated people use simulated equipment in a simulated environment. Online simulation web sites allows trainees to conduct and perform actual experiments.

The use of simulated activities in training is becoming common. Following are some advantages of using simulations in education and training:

(i) Simulations give hands-on experience so that trainees become participants, not just listeners or observers.

(ii) Simulations are virtually real; they simulate some activity so well that real learning takes place.

(iii) Simulations motivate the learners as it involves them in the learning activity.

(iv) Simulations can be designed so that they can take age into consideration

(v) Simulations can be designed so that learner's inputs can be embedded into the learning activities.

Q15. Discuss the concept of computer mediated communication.

Ans. Computer-mediated Communication (CMC) is defined as any communicative transaction that occurs through the use of two or more networked computers. Popular forms of CMC include email, video, audio or text chat, bulletin boards, list-services and MMOs (massively multiplayer online game). These settings are changing rapidly with the development of new technologies. Computer-mediated Communication is a system consisting of human and computer, which means that it is alive instead of some rigid facilities.

The participation of humans makes themselves creators, users, ameliorators, furthermore the core of the computer-mediated communication system, which means that without humans, the system would only have cold apparatus left. The combination of humans and computers, or to say networks, forms a complicated information transmitting system aiming at information exchanging and sharing freely. There are some general features of information system in the Computer-mediated Communication System, together with some special features of human social system.

The networks or computers operating in different platforms are connected to Internet by a common protocol known as Transmission Control Protocol/Internet Protocol (TCP/IP), which provides different services, like:

- **Electronic Mail (E-Mail):** permits the user to send and receive messages electronically to an individual or a group. In the next section you can read more about it.
- **USENET or Views and News:** is the BBS (Bulletin Board Service) of Internet. The messages in the BBS are organised into thousands of News groups, which cover specific areas of interest.
- **TELNET or Remote Login:** Telnet allows an Internet user to access a remote host. After properly connecting and logging into the remote host, the user can enter data, run programs or carry out other operations.
- **File Transfer Protocol (FTP):** It permits an Internet user to move or transfer a file from one computer to another even if they are running on different platform (or operating system). The files may have data, graphics, text, etc.
- **Internet Navigators:** Everyday more and more new users are using the Internet, a global information ocean. There are several powerful tools used on Internet for searching for information. These information-tracking or searching utilities are means to develop easy methods of discovering, locating, and retrieving information on various objects freely available on the Internet.

Besides of above mentioned facilities, cmc provides following facilities also:

- **World Wide Web (WWW):** The Web is a means of transmitting data through the Internet by using a protocol called Hyper Text Transfer Protocol (HTTP). The Web browsers, like Internet Explorer, Mozilla or Netscape, are used to access web pages. The Web page can contain text, graphics, audio and video. A Web page may have *web-links* that take you to other Web pages, recorded sounds, or digital video clips. Mosaic was the first web browser that displayed graphics, sound and video clips on a web page. In past years, Internet Explorer and

Netscape were the most popular browsers available, but new browsers are being created. Today, browsers such as Firefox, Mozila are becoming increasingly popular.

- **Email:** One of the most valuable features of communicating via email is that it is asynchronous, meaning the recipient need not be at a computer to receive the message you send. The message will be stored and available to be read when the recipient is ready to read it. In order to send and receive email, you must have access to an Email account. E-mail vendors like Hotmail, Yahoo, MSN, Google (G-mail), Rediffmail are common. E-Mail vendors are continuously coming up with their new versions of E-Mail systems. Let us discuss a few important aspects of a good E-mail system. The E-Mail should contain the feature to compose and send messages easily. Message editing and the ability to easily send attachments that can be quickly opened and read by the recipient are important for the user of an E-Mail system. Also, it should have good amount of storage capacity to store your valuable mails. However, an E-Mail system can do more than just send message back and forth.
- **Online-Chatting:** Online chat and messaging services are free on Internet, however some service providers also have paid services. There are many Internet users replacing traditional conversation with online chat. Online chat is steadily replacing telephony as the means of office and home communication. Now a days, mobile/handheld devices are also providing the technology for online chat. Online chat can refer to any kind of communication over Internet, but is primarily meant to refer to direct one-on-one chat or text-based group chat (formally also known as synchronous conferencing), using tools such as instant messaging applications-like Rediff, yahoo, and MSN chat applications.
- **Electronic Discussion Groups:** There are a variety of electronic discussion groups on the Internet like yahoo, Google and MSN groups. These groups are generally created to share information, communicate ideas, ask questions and solve problems on specific topics. Messages are communicated over the email address, and also through the group home page.

Some groups are moderated, and the messages that are added to the list and distributed to the group are monitored. Some groups are unmediated and every message submitted is included.

- **Blogging:** Blogging is gaining popularity in education, as it removes the technical barriers of writing and publishing online, which encourages students to keep a record of their ideas and thinking over time. Blogging also facilitate readers to give critical feedback on any topic. Readers can add comments, where readers can be teachers, students or others. Trainers today realise the potential of blogs, media-sharing services and other social software, which can be used to create new learning opportunities. Trainees can also use blogs as they can provide a personal space online, to ask questions, comment on other questions, publish work, and link to other web sources. However a blog need not be restricted to a single author, it can merge different kinds of ideas, including fellow students, teachers, and subject specialists. An example: http://edu.blogs.com/
- **VOIP:** One advantage of VoIP is that the calls over the Internet do not gain a surcharge beyond what you are paying for Internet access, in the same way as we don't pay for sending individual e-mails over the Internet. VoIP services can operate over computer or a special VoIP phone. However some services use a traditional phone connected to a VoIP adapter. VoIP services transform voice into a digital signal that travels over the Internet. If you are calling a regular phone number, the signal is converted to a regular telephone signal (called as analog signal) before it reaches the destination. Merging voice and data networks opens up a world of opportunities for better interaction between teachers, students and specialists.
- **Podcasting:** Podcasting is similar to a radio broadcast but the files are available for downloading from a website. Podcasting has become a popular technology in education, in part because it provides a way of delivering educational content to learners. The main advantage is that the users have full control over what, where and when they access the files. However, to

operate properly we need sufficient bandwidth and podcasting is not designed for two-way interaction or teacher-student/trainee simultaneous participation.

Q16. What is the role of IT in self-learning and training? Discuss the advantages of self-learning using information technology.

Ans. Information Technology will keep on changing the elaboration, acquisition and transmission of knowledge; thus the implementing and promotion of training programs to develop skills and abilities related to the proper use of technology focused on self-learning.

Information Technology (IT) should be used to support learning/training rather that just an information provider. We must evolve and design better environments where IT can be used as facilitators for learning and knowledge building.

The increasing requirement for lifelong self-learning can be supported by an IT infrastructure. Technology cannot teach learners. However, learners should utilise the technologies to teach themselves and others. Learning will result when technologies involve learners in knowledge building, sharing, and its expression. There are following methods which we use for educational purpose:

(1) Online Simulations and Interactive Tools: These methods allow learners/trainees to experience real objects and events. Interactive tools allow students to engage multiple learning styles in the completion of individual or group activities. In addition, sound, video, animation and other multimedia features appeal to multiple learning styles and capture the learner's attention. Online interactive simulations have a friendly role in the learning process than that which simply provides a practice environment. Also, online feedback can be delivered based upon the responses and actions of the learner in the simulation or interactive tools. It provides a continuously monitored and guided environment by an area expert. Practical learning thus made possible can provide the learner with an opportunity to add to the theoretical concepts.

(2) Online Collaborative Communication: These methods are useful and supportive in construction of knowledge through collaborative communication. For example, online chatting, blogging, online groups, discussion forum etc. help in the communication process.

Advantages of self-learning using information technology: The main advantages of self-learning using information technology are as follows:

(1) Learner can access the specific area or topic s/he needs rather than doing the complete course with a generic and broad framework.

(2) Using IT, these self-learning programs can be customised to each individual's needs, One can learn and evaluate him/herself when and where the learner is comfortable according to one's personal schedule, with instantaneous results and feedback.

(3) Everyone can access repositories of self-learning materials, easily retrieving earlier lessons, updating skills, or selecting from among different teaching methods in order to discover the most effective ways of learning.

(4) It is Any-Time-Learning like Any-Time-Money (ATM). You may use Self Learning materials online at home or in the office, anytime. Any individual can participate in self-learning training programs regardless of geographic location.

(5) It allows us to learn in a collaborative way, where we share experiences and can take guidance from experts and teachers.

Q17. Write the steps for designing a training programme.

Ans. A training programme whether to be delivered in a face to face mode or online has to be designed appropriately. This involves the following steps:

- **Step One: Need Assessment:** the needs of the employees in the present global scenario may or may not match the ground realities of the organisation. For instance teachers abroad are developing skills to prepare multimedia packages at their work stations but in view of the infrastructure and financial resources, the same may not be possible in every institution. Hence, the trainers need to strike a balance between needs and realities and then make realistic assessments.
- **Step Two:** Set goals, set objectives for the training programme to stay focused and allow evaluation later.
- **Step Three:** Develop a training plan as per the needs assessed, objectives, policies of the organisation. The mode of imparting training i.e. through face-to-face mode with or without technological support/online has to be decided. The choice of

technology is also to be spelt out. Other factors like duration, venue, etc. are to be planned. Whether training would be for groups or on an individual basis also has to be decided.

For training programmes imparted to distant trainees whether online or through audio/video/multimedia CDS the content has to be so designed that it is in the form of self learning material and also has provisions for evaluation and feedback. The designing of the content has been discussed in details in the third unit of the course, MES034.

- **Step Four:** Implementation of the training programme as per the schedule developed.
- **Step Five:** Evaluation both formative i.e. assessing during the programme through periodic assessment and summative, i.e. to assess the learning outcome as well as adequacy of inputs like method of teaching, experiences imparted, time devoted, etc. at the end of the programme is important. Through evaluation it is ascertained whether the objectives for the training programme framed earlier have been fulfilled or not.

Q18. Discuss how in various areas of education ICT can be implemented.

Ans. Implementation of technology based training programme requires a lot of planning. It included assessment and formulation of objectives, the programme has to be planned for the timing, content, selection of appropriate technology, resource person/experts, designing issues if delivered in distance mode, evaluation, etc. Even while it is being implemented, monitoring is required on a continuous basis to ensure that it does not get derailed. Formative evaluation has to be done to assess learning outcomes. It is very important for a teacher/trainer to understand how ICT technologies can be useful in different areas. Various fields of education are as follows:

(1) Mathematics: There are numerous ways for applying ICT in mathematics to motivate students and to demonstrate the utility of mathematics in real life. These ways are as follows:

(i) **Spreadsheets:** It can be useful in mathematics. From calculations to showing patterns in certain number manipulations. With spreadsheets, one can manipulate variables or parameters to observe certain properties clearly and promptly. Learners can also ask for different types of charts to be plotted from data in a spreadsheet. Teachers can design templates which have values previously entered in order to demonstrate effects from changing variables. At a more advanced level, spreadsheets can be designed by students themselves in order to help to solve realistic and contextual problems.

(ii) **Modeling and Simulation:** Learners can use simple modeling packages, such as Mathematical and MATLAB to gain insight into mathematical functions. Graphic calculators can also be used for this reason. Modeling and simulation can also be used with special software for geometry to give students a better understanding of figures in 2 or 3-dimensional space.

(iii) **Internet:** Learners can utilise applets that are freely available on the Internet for performing different mathematical activities and solving certain mathematical problems.

(2) Sciences: Some of the areas in which training may be required so that ICT can be used effectively in the teaching of science subjects (Physics, Chemistry, Biology, Geography etc.) are illustrated through the following examples.

(i) **Databases:** Databases can be useful for storing variables such as the characteristics of chemical elements in the periodic table, characteristics of plants, insects, and mammals; and then interrogate these databases to find relationships and commonalties.

(ii) **Spreadsheets:** Spreadsheets can be used to tabulate and calculate results of experiments. The use of spreadsheets is a better way to demonstrate how changing a particular variable gives definite effects. Its implementation in natural science is similar to mathematics; various types of charts can be plotted and we can also design templates that have values already entered to illustrate effects of manipulating variables.

(iii) **Internet:** It is useful in communication with other students/teachers. In research or project assignments, information accessible on the Internet can be used. Online data can be downloaded and shared with others. In addition to this, readily available easy-to-use applets to simulate all types of natural processes can be used. Hence, training to use the Internet is needed.

(iv) **Word processing and presentation:** These softwares can be used in preparing learning/training resources, reports and presentations on the results of experiments or research. Learners can add ready-to-use graphics, or graphics that they create themselves. They can also use data and graphs created from measurement software.

(v) **Modeling and Simulation:** A natural calamity like the Tsunami can be simulated in classrooms without any danger to participants. Dissecting animals can also be demonstrated through simulation. When learners have performed or have witnessed a demonstration, repeating the experience through modeling will give them further insight into the roles of variables and parameters in a process.

(3) Art: ICT can be used in numerous ways in subjects like art, music and dance.

(i) **Music and dance Tools:** ICT can modify the course of music in many attractive ways. Software tools give students the opportunity of composing and performing music themselves without having troubles with technical characteristics of notation or playing an instrument. In dance as in music, there is a variety of user-friendly software for designing simple choreographs to assist students learn to perform.

(ii) **Graphical package:** A few graphics packages allow for the making of artwork. However, art teachers are normally more concerned in the method in which students can make patterns, matching patterns, and patterns with diversity. In textile design, for example, students can give a better result overall with limited exertion with computers. In the design of posters and other printed matter, more complex graphical software ensures a specialised product in least time, with the option to reuse a design. Training in these areas are hence needed.

(4) ICT in Evaluation: Spreadsheets are useful tools for individual or group work, and are widely used in education and commerce. Simple software spreadsheet packages can be used in classroom as productivity tools. Here is an example which demonstrates that how we can use a spreadsheet to evaluate the students' performance in a class.

Example: We have a class with five students during the academic session, and a total of six evaluation activities are to be conducted including quiz, lab and written test, based on which the total marks and percentage need to be calculated.

We have taken MS-Excel, as a spreadsheet tool for evaluating our class. First of all we enter the values in the Excel sheet as shown in the figure given below, then using the function 'SUM' we calculate the marks of each component for students. We can calculate the percentage also using the total marks and maximum marks. Using the graph utility you can generate the graph for the students' performance as shown in the figure given below. Further using pie chart option in graphs we can also present a list of students with marks in certain ranges. As in this example we can see that 2 people are having marks between 70 and 75, one is having marks between 75 and 80, and two people are having marks more than 80 marks. Similarly some other simple to complex calculation can be done through MS-Excel spreadsheet tool.

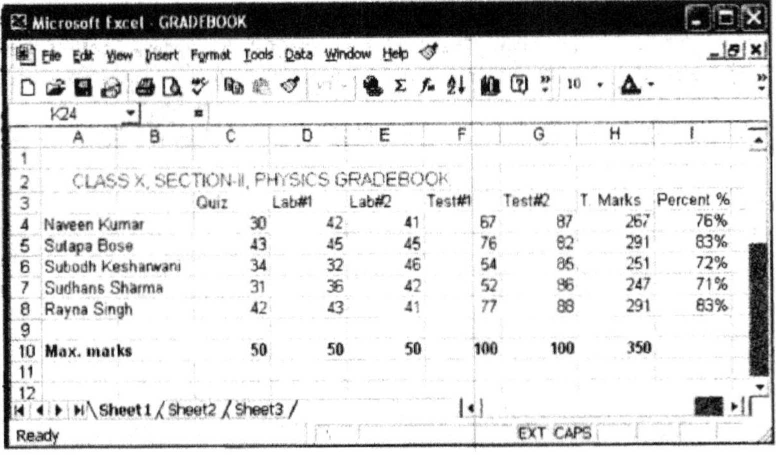

CLASS X, SECTION-II, PHYSICS GRADEBOOK

	Quiz	Lab#1	Lab#2	Test#1	Test#2	T. Marks	Percent %
Naveen Kumar	30	42	41	67	87	267	76%
Sulapa Bose	43	45	45	76	82	291	83%
Subodh Kesharwani	34	32	46	54	85	251	72%
Sudhans Sharma	31	36	42	52	86	247	71%
Rayna Singh	42	43	41	77	88	291	83%
Max. marks	**50**	**50**	**50**	**100**	**100**	**350**	

Fig. 2.2: Excel Sheet showing students marks in different components, with total marks and their percentage

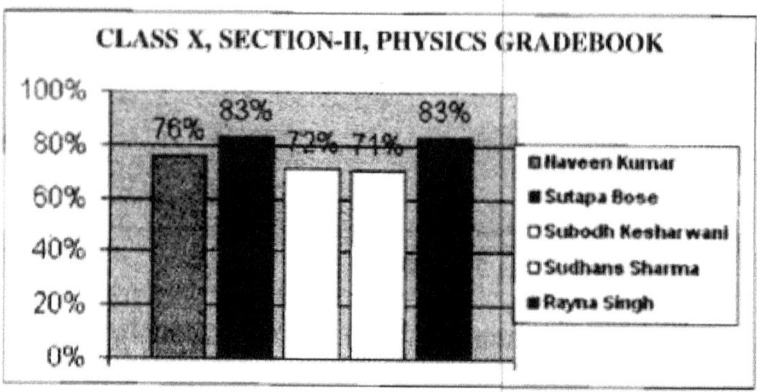

Fig. 2.3: Graphical Presentation of students' percentage

We thus see that teachers need to be trained in the use of ET for teaching effectively in today's Information age. Evaluation component is also designed by framing multiple choice and other types of questions, quizzes, etc. They can be scored and feedback is given. Through hyperlinks, the learner may navigate to the right answer or explanation about the answer or relevant portion of the content for rereading.

❑❑❑

Chapter-3

Print Media

Q1. What is learning? Discuss the factors which affect the process of learning.

Ans. Learning may be defined as "any relatively permanent change in behaviour or behavioural potential produced by experience". The term "relatively (more or less) permanent change" implies that a change in behaviour must last a fairly long period. Behavioural changes that occur due to learning are relatively permanent. They must be distinguished from the behavioural changes that are neither permanent nor learned.

The nature of learning is purposeful and goal-directed. Without any aim or motivation, it is highly difficult to learn anything. For example, if one wants to be a software expert his/her learning efforts would be different from those of the person who wants to learn law. Learning is transferable. When we get advantage of one learned skill or experience in another related area this is regarded as transfer of learning. For example, mathematical abilities help in learning physical sciences. However, it has also been evident in some instances that learning of one thing hinders to learning of another. For example learning two foreign languages at the same time may create confusion and interfere with the learning of these languages

There are following factors which affect learning process:

(1) Environment: The learning environment refers to conditions external to the learner, including the nature of the skill, performance elements, practice methods and feedback. The learning environment can have a positive and negative impact on the learning process and is a major factor in the development of skills. The learning environment refers to everything outside the learner, including the weather, the skill itself, the situation it is practiced in, and information from coaches.

(2) Characteristics of the Learner: When it comes to learning, characteristics of learners affect how they are motivated to learn. By appealing to the unique qualities of learners, we can design more effective and motivating study materials. The age of learners, intelligence level, mental abilities level of aspiration, anxieties, resources available, physical conditions etc., have a great significant effect on learning.

- **Nature of the Learning Material:** Textbooks and other instructional materials have a direct impact on what is taught in schools and how it is taught. If one is going through difficult and meaningless material (content) s/he might face hurdles in learning that material. On the other hand, it is easier to learn clear, familiar, logical and meaningful material. So there is always a need for a mechanism to review and control the quality of learning materials used in classrooms with regard to relevance, content, educational approach and efficacy, as well as to ensure that the provision of learning materials reflects government policies.
- **Interest and motivation:** Motivation can be described as a state that energizes, directs and sustains behavior. Motivation involves goals and requires activity. Goals provide the impetus for and the direction of action. While action entails effort, persistence in order to sustain activity for a long period of time. For instance, if the student wants to be a physician or work in the medical field, they may be driven by it as an attainable goal. As a result, they may want to invest all of their free time in getting to the next level. If they want to get into the top schools, they will also seek to achieve the highest grades. Whatever the individual's motivation factor is, it is clear that motivation and learning will often go hand in hand.
- **Practice:** To learn and improve skills, practice is required. There are a number of different ways in which skill practice sessions can be conducted such as massed or distributed, and whole or part. Active practice or rehearsal improves retention, and distributed practice is usually more effective than massed practice. The advantage to distributed practice is especially

noticeable for lists, fast presentation rates or unfamiliar stimulus material. The advantage to distributed practice apparently occurs because massed practice allows the learner to associate a word with only a single context, but distributed practice allows association with many different contexts.

- • **Learning Method:** There are many learning methods. Which method we choose and use also affects our learning. Some of the popular learning methods are: part V/s. whole method (learning a content part by part as against trying to learn the whole thing), active V/s. passive (learning by understanding the content as against learning by rote), rhythmical method (making a rhyme out of the learning material as rhymes are easier to learn and are also retained), learning by association, trial and error, imitation, observation, insight, etc. If the method of learning involves understanding, it will lead to efficient learning.

Q2. Describe various theories of learning and their educational implications.

Ans. Learning is one of the most important activities of living beings. It is at the very core of the educational process, although most of what people learn occurs outside of school. For thousands of years, philosophers and psychologists have sought to understand the nature of learning, how it occurs, and how one person can influence the learning of another person through teaching and similar endeavors. Various theories of learning have been suggested, and these theories differ for a variety of reasons. These learning theories not only describe and explain the necessary conditions under which learning takes place but also emphasises what takes place when effective learning occurs. Different views of learning theories have been discussed as follows:

(1) Behaviouristic theory of learning: The term "Behaviorism" is primarily concerned with observable and measurable aspects of human behavior. In defining behavior, behaviorist learning theories emphasize changes in behavior that result from stimulus-response associations made by the learner. Behavior is directed by stimuli. An individual selects one response instead of another because of prior conditioning and psychological drives existing at the moment of the action.

Behaviorists assert that the only behaviors worthy of study are those that can be directly observed; thus, it is actions, rather than thoughts or emotions, which are the legitimate object of study. Behaviorist theory does not explain abnormal behavior in terms of the brain or its inner workings. Rather, it posits that all behavior is learned habits, and attempts to account for how these habits are formed.

In education, advocates of behaviorism have effectively adopted this system of rewards and punishments in their classrooms by rewarding desired behaviors and punishing inappropriate ones. Rewards vary, but must be important to the learner in some way. For example, if a teacher wishes to teach the behavior of remaining seated during the class period, the successful student's reward might be checking the teacher's mailbox, running an errand, or being allowed to go to the library to do homework at the end of the class period. As with all teaching methods, success depends on each student's stimulus and response, and on associations made by each learner. There are following different theories of behaviourism which studies connection of S-R:

(i) **Thorndike's Trial and Error Theory:** E.L. Thorndike (1874-1949) was the chief exponent of the theory of connectionism or trial and error. The basis of learning accepted by Thorndike is an association between the sense impressions and impulses to action. This association came to be known as a 'bond' or a 'connection'. Since it is these bonds or connections which become strengthened or weakened in the making and breaking of habits, Thorndike's system is sometimes and response type of learning, it is also called S.R. Psychology of Learning. Thorndike called it learning by selecting and connecting. It is also known as trial and error theory as learning takes place through random repetitions.

Thorndike propounded his theory on the basis of experiments conducted on cats, chickens, dogs, fish, monkeys and rats. He placed them under different learning situations and studied them carefully. With the help of these experiments, he tried to evolve certain laws and evolved his theory of connectionism or trial and error. It interesting to know the type experiment he performed with these animals. Illustration, of his experiments:

Thorndike named the learning of his experimental cat as "Trial and Error Learning". He maintained that the learning is nothing but the stamping in of the correct responses and stamping out of the incorrect responses through trial and error. In trying for the correct solution the cat made so many vain attempts. It committed error after error before gaining success. On subsequent trials, it tried to avoid the erroneous ways and repeat the correct way of manipulation the latch. Thorndike called it "Learning by selecting and connecting" as it provides an opportunity for the selection of the proper responses and correct or associate them with adequate stimuli. In this reference, Thorndike has written– "Learning is connecting. The mind is man's connection system."

On the basis of his experiments, Thorndike propounded the following laws of learning:

(a) **The Law of Readiness:** The law states, "When any conduction unit is ready to conduct, for it to do so is satisfying. When any conduction unit is not in readiness to conduct, for it to conduct is annoying. When any conduction unit is in readiness to conduct, for it not to do so is annoying."

The law is indicative of learner's state to participate in the learning process. According to Thorndike, readiness is preparation for action. Readiness does not come automatically with maturation. It is a law of preparatory adjustment, not a law about growth. Thorndike termed the neurons and synapses involved in establishment of a specific bond or connection, a conduction unit. According to this law, for a conduction unit ready to conduct, to do, is satisfying and for it not to do so is annoying.

(b) **The Law of Effect:** The law states, "Of several responses made to the same situation, those which are accompanied or closely followed by satisfaction to the animal will, other things being equal, be more firmly connected with the situation, so that, when it recurs, they will be more likely to recur, those which are accompanied or closely followed by discomfort to the animal, will, other things being equal, have 'their' connection with that situation weakened, so that, when it recurs, they will be less likely to occur. The greater the satisfaction or discomfort, the greater the strengthening or weakening of the bond."

Thorndike explains the meaning of satisfaction and discomfort as: "By a satisfying sate of affairs is meant one which the animal does nothing to avoid, often doing such things as attain and preserve it. By a discomforting or annoying state of affairs is meant one which the animal commonly avoids and abandons."

(c) **The Law of Exercise or Repetition.** It states, "Any response to a situation will, other things being equal, be more strongly connected with the situation in proportion to the number of times it has been connected with that situation and to the average vigour and duration of the connection."

According to this law, the more a stimulus-induced response is repeated, the longer it will be retained. The law states, other things being equal, exercise strengthens the bond between situation and response. Conversely a bond is weakened through failure to exercise it. Thus the law has two subparts, (a) law of use, and (b) law of disuse.

Law of Use-"When a modifiable connection is made between a situation and response that connection's strength is, other things being equal, increased."

Law of Disuse- "When a modifiable connection is not made between a situation and response, during a length of time, that connection's strength is decreased.

E.L. Thorndike (1874-1949) was the chief exponent of the theory of connectionism of trial and error. The basis of learning accepted by Thorndike is an association between the sense impressions and impulses to action. This association came to be known as a 'bond' or a 'connection'. Since it is these bonds or connections which become strengthened or weakened in the making and breaking of habits, Thorndike's system is sometimes called a 'bond' psychology or simply 'connectionism'. As it believes in stimulus and response type of learning, it is also called S.R. Psychology of Learning. Thorndike called it learning by connecting. It is also trial and error theory as learning takes place through random repetitions.

Thorndike propounded his theory on the basis of experiments conducted on cats, chickens, dogs, fish, monkeys and rats. He placed them under different learning situations and studied them carefully. With the help of these experiments, he tried to evolve certain laws and evolved his theory of connectionism or trial and error. It is interesting to know the type of experiments he performed with these animals. Illustration, of his experiments:

Thorndike named the learning of his experimental cat as "Trial and Error Learning". He maintained that the learning is nothing but the stamping in of the correct responses and stamping out of the incorrect responses through trial and error. In trying for the correct solution the cat made so many vain attempts. It committed error after error before gaining success. On subsequent trials, it tried to avoid the erroneous ways and repeat the correct way of manipulating the latch. Thorndike called it "Learning by selecting and connecting" as it provides an opportunity for the selection of the proper responses and correct or associate them with adequate stimuli. In this reference, Thorndike has written – "Learning is connecting. The mind is man's connection system.

(ii) Pavlov's classical conditioning theory: The Pavlovian theory of behaviourism is also known as *classical conditioning* or *respondent behaviour* or *Pavlovian conditioning.* Its pioneer was Ivan Pavlov (1849-1936) by profession was a physiologist. These are the responses that occur due to external stimulus. For example, Salivation, knee jerk, blinking of the eye, etc. The external stimulation can be the smell/sight of food, tapping of the patellar tendon, puffing of air, etc.

Under neutral condition, a dog salivates only when it smells/eats meat. This is an unconditioned response (UR). Meat is also an example of unconditioned stimulus (US). The dog salivates automatically (this is due to the activity of the dog's autonomic nervous system-AVS). In actuality during conditioning, the original response to the US is designated as UR; the learnt behaviour to the conditioned stimulus (CS) is called a conditioned response (CR).

Application of the laws of classical conditioning: Psychologists consider classical conditioning as a simple form of learning, yet, it depends on some principles:

(a) **Acquisition:** Presentation of the CS and US is called a trial and time taken by the animal in establishing an association between the CS and CR is called the acquisition stage of conditioning. Pavlov had encountered three temporal relations in conditioning experiments, which are given as follows:

- Simultaneous conditioning, the bell (CS) is terminated after a fraction of a second before the meat powder (UR) is presented and it stays until the dog has salivated.
- Delayed conditioning, the bell is rung for several seconds or more before the meat powder (UR) is presented and it is made to exist till the response (salivation) occurs.
- Trace conditioning, the bell (CS) is rung first and then it is extinguished before meat powder (US) is produced. This procedure only develops a memory trace of the bell, i.e. the CS remains to be conditioned.

(b) **Extinction:** Repetition of the conditioned stimulus without reinforcement is called extinction. Fourth non-reinforcement trial had produced only about three drops of saliva by the dog. Ringing of bell without meat powder gradually failed to produce any salivation in the dog by the end of the ninth non-reinforced trial.

(c) **Stimulus generalisation:** Pavlov also discovered that the dog could be conditioned to salivate by the use of a flash of light and/or the beat of a metronome. It means, the dog tended to generalised the conditioned response to other stimuli as well that were similar to the original conditioned response. The principle of similarity forms the basis of generalisation among the conditioned stimuli.

A dog has been conditioned to salivate to the sound of tuning fork say of 300 wavelength will also salivate to a tuning fork having a wavelength of 275 or 325. The more of similarity between the new and original conditioning stimuli, the more is the likelihood of evoking the conditioned response.

(d) **Discrimination:** In an experiment, the experimenter, on some trials, paired a stimulus called CS+ with an unconditioned stimulus. On the other trials, another stimulus is called the CS, was presented only without the unconditioned stimulus. The result of this experiment has been given below:

- The CS + is paired with an unconditioned stimulus;
- The CS – (another stimulus) remains unpaired;
- Due to more and more trial runs, CS + elicits strong conditioned responses; and
- Only very weak/little conditioning is elicited by the CS.

(e) **Spontaneous recovery:** Pavlov after achieving conditioning extinguished it. After a few trials, conditioned salivary response had ceased completely. The dog was then moved out of the laboratory and a rest of 24 hours was allowed. When the dog was tested after the rest, the conditioned response immediately appeared on the first presentation of the conditioned stimulus. This effect is designated as spontaneous recovery. The conditioned response occurs after a period of rest.

(iii) Skinner's operant conditioning theory: The *Skinnerian theory* of behaviourism is also known as the theory of *Operant*

Conditioning or Instrumental Behaviour or Skinnerian conditioning. Its pioneer was E. L. Thorndike and B. F. Skinner. They occur due to the consequence of an action produce by the animal (human being also come under this category) to deal with environment. It is mediated by the Central Nervous System (CNS) of the organism.

Operant conditioning (or instrumental conditioning) is a type of learning in which an individual's behaviour is modified by its antecedents and consequences. It is a method of learning that occurs through rewards and punishments for behaviour. Through operant conditioning, an association is made between a behaviour and a consequence for that behaviour.

In the late 1930s, Skinner (a Harvard psychologist) created the operant box. It is a simple box in which the animal is reinforced by providing a food pallet/water arrangement. Hence, positive reinforcement enhances the lever pressing (rat). The lever (the CS) is presented just before the food pallet, i.e. the US, and then it is withheld until the next trial.

Educational implications of Stimulus-Response theory: The S-R approach to learning has very wide implications. Mainly these theories emphasise providing a conductive and supportive environment to facilitate the learning with intelligently manipulated reinforcements. Basic principles emphasising the implications of the behaviuorist views are as follows:

(i) Readiness helps learning: Teacher should prepare the minds of the students to be ready to accept the knowledge, skills and aptitudes. For this, he should provide opportunities for those experiences in which students can spontaneously participate. In other words, he should arouse their capacity to link the experiences with their everyday life. 'Simple to complex' is the important maxim. Aptitude tests may be given to the students to find out their readiness to learn.

(ii) Practice leads to perfection: For acquiring any skill a learner needs frequent repetition or practice. So more and more opportunities should be provided to the students to use and repeat the experiences they get in the classroom. Drill strengthens the bonds of S-R. Review of the lesson maintains connections.

(iii) The learners should be active: As has been observed repeatedly, learning is an active process. Hence, for effective learning, the learners should be active. "Learning by doing" is the best technique for effective learning.

(iv) Satisfaction facilitates learning: Learning takes place properly when it results in satisfaction and the learner derives pleasure out of it. In the situation when the child meets a failure or gets dissatisfaction, the progress in learning is blocked. All the pleasant experiences have a lasting influence and are remembered for a long time, while the unpleasant ones are soon forgotten. Therefore, the satisfaction or dissatisfaction, pleasure or displeasure obtained as a result of some learning ensures the degree of effectiveness of that learning.

(v) Appropriate reinforcement should be there: There are many types of reinforcements. If you want to strengthen the behaviour, you should apply certain type of reinforcements like praise, reward, a nod, etc. And if you want to weaken some behaviour, then different type of reinforcers should be used. The clues and model answers at the end of the units give you the feedback and reinforce your answers.

(2) Cognitive theory of learning: The cognitive theory is a theoretical perspective in which learning by observing others is the focus of study.

The cognitivist revolution replaced behaviorism is 1960s as the dominant paradigm. Cognitivism focuses on the inner mental activities – opening the "black box" of the human mind is valuable and necessary for understanding how people learn. Mental processes such as thinking, memory, knowing, and problem-solving need to be explored. Knowledge can be seen as schema or symbolic mental constructions. Learning is defined as change in a learner's schemata.

A response to behaviorism, people are not "programmed animals" that merely respond to environmental stimuli; people are rational beings that require active participation in order to learn, and whose actions are a consequence of thinking. Changes in behavior are observed, but only as an indication of what is occurring in the learner's head. Cognitivism uses Changes in behavior are observed, but only as an indication of what is occurring in the learner's head. Cognitivism uses the metaphor of the mind as computer. information comes in, is being processed, and leads to certain outcomes.

Educational Implications of cognitive theory:

(i) **Responses are influenced by the total situation:** The teachers and trainers should always keep in mind that they themselves, learners, and the activities performed, all from the learning environment. All these essential components of learning environment influence learning.

(ii) **Goal setting:** Goal setting is highly important step in learning. It is this stage, which would determine and predict success or failure. Also, it provides the learners with the motivation.

(iii) **Insight develops according to age:** As we mature and gain experience, we develop an insight. So, the teachers must select problem situations according to the learner's mental level.

(iv) **The arrangement of a problem situation affects insight:** It has been observed that the perception of relationships among the variables of a situation lead to a solution. The learners should be provided with structured learning problem so that the relationships are perceived clearly.

(v) **Insightful solutions are transferable:** Once the solution is reached, this experience can be easily utilized in similar problem situations including new problem situations. For instance, one who drives a two wheeler on a busy road finds driving a car easy.

(vi) **Encouraging learning with understanding:** Rote learning or learning by formula soon fades but learning through understanding lasts long.

(vii) **Providing cognitive feedback:** As has been seen previously, feedback not only indicates our direction (we are on the right path or not) of learning but also serves as reinforcement for further and self-directed learning.

Q3. What are the characteristics of adult learning?

Ans. Variability is a key factor in adults' learning. In the past, it was often assumed that all adults would learn in the same way. Current theories of adult learning reflect the understanding that adults learn in many different ways for many different reasons. Because of this, it is very important that adult education programmes should be learner-centred.

Adult learning is recognised as a form of participation in social practices. This means that learning occurs in all contexts of people's lives. Learning is not just about behaviour and cognitive processing, current research findings emphasise the importance of using the life experiences and life roles of adult learners and suggest that learning develops as adults engage in interactions with other people and with their social environment.

(1) Adults have concrete and immediate needs: Adults are more aware of their immediate needs. Instead of lengthy theoretical discourses, practical problems and their solutions are preferred. The content has to be more task or problem-centered and above all need based.

(2) Adults go for Voluntary Education: Age not only brings maturity but also responsibilities with it. That is why they show increased readiness for learning and education than children do.

(3) Intrinsic motivation of adults is high: Adults may lack time but are more motivated to learn than children. External rewards are not so motivating for the adult learners as the internal incentives and curiosity to learn more. The usefulness and appropriateness of the material to be learned directly affect their motivation and interest to learn.

(4) Maintaining adults' interest in studies is challenging: There are a lot of factors like family pressures, social and job commitments that influence the motivation and interest of the adult learners.

(5) Adult learners are mature people: Adults are mature unlike children. They are self-reliant learners and they like determining their own learning pace. They have realistic and useful past experiences and insights about what might lead them to success. They prefer a democratic, participatory, and collaborative environment for learning.

(6) Adults long for control over learning content, activities and pace of learning: Adults require active involvement in determining how and what they will learn. They desire some control over their learning content, activities, pace of learning and working environments.

(7) Helping adults evaluate themselves: Scope for self evaluation challenges and motivates adults and if followed by constructive feedback, learning is facilitated.

Q4. Explain essential guidelines that have to be considered while designing learning material in the print medium.

Or

"We should design our material in such a way that it not only facilitates learning but also increases and maintains interest and motivation of learners." Discuss the statement in the context of printed learning materials.

Ans. Properly designed course materials create and maintain interest and motivation of the learners. the physical layout of printed material and the organisation of the content, besides the nature of the information provided, highly influence the learning environment. So we need to follow following guidelines for designing course materials:

(1) Content: The instructions provided should be clear and specific. It should be interesting to sustain attention. Scope for further learning should be ensured through a list of suggested readings. Scope for practice should also be kept in view. All these features will keep the learner active.

(2) Textual Unity: If there is no textual unity in the lesson, it distracts the learners from learning. The content should be supported with the relevant headings and subheadings to highlight the structuring of the text. Further, the graphical presentation should be in consistency with the information being delivered.

(3) Meaningful: The content should be meaningful to the learners. Hence, the language should be lucid and there should be amply illustration and examples. Chadwick (1990) rightly suggests that materials should be designed as "an interactive medium which provides information, then stimulates and facilitates the successful processing of the information."

(4) Organization of materials: It is important to organize the learning material logically and it should flow systematically and logically from that starting point which is clearly related to the learners' past experiences. Breaking down the message and information into smaller pieces under logical and relevant headings makes the material eye catching, easier to understand, learn and manage. There should be enough scope for the mental exercises of the learners and the text should contain cognitive links pointing both and forward. Also, within the text, there should be occasional breaks where the learners could review the material they have been studying (Orna, 1985).

(5) Purpose: The first and most important things is that, instead of just directly getting started with the material-writing, you should have a clear vision of what your basic purpose behind developing this course is, what you want to achieve by developing this course, and what you want to convey. This will set the goal (objectives as mentioned at the beginning of the unit) for learning. Goal oriented learning is more focused.

(6) Learner Characteristics: You should also explore in advance before developing learning materials and seek information from prospective learners about their previous knowledge, present demands, their mental level readiness, etc. The text should also avoid anything that could hurt someone's feelings.

(7) Learner-Based Approach: The course development is to be learner-centered, and take care of the learner's particular needs and aspirations. The learners are to be encouraged to develop analytical and critical thinking and cognitive skills through suitable activities and questions.

(8) Feedback: Providing feedback is highly crucial so that the learners might also judge the adequacy of their responses. The mechanism of feedback works on the following grounds that it not only indicates to the learners the wrong and right answers but also how they could reach right answers and improve them. It enables self-evaluation and self-assessment of performance. And above all, feedback and positive reinforcement motivate self-directed learning.

(9) Assessment: Assessment is the most important activity for any type of learning. It assesses and reveals whether the learners have acquired the capability or competence you desired to develop in them through your course. In text questions should be included so that learners can assess their own understanding, learning and progress. Activities can generate scope for reflection and even practical training.

Q5. Write an essay on the origin and development of print medium and explain its relevance in distance education.

Ans. Communication is a fundamental process without which neither can humans lead a smooth life nor a society can grow. Even the prosperity of a society is judged by the extent to which its members afford and make use of various means of communication.

Print media has initiated the process of communication, since the Chinese first invented the art of printing. They made wooden blocks to print letters. This was started during the period of the Tang Dynasty in 600 AD. The oldest known surviving printed work in a woodblock is a Buddhist scripture of 684 AD. It is now exhibited in a calligraphy museum in Tokyo, the capital of Japan.

The first printed book published in China was the Buddhist text, the "Diamond Sutra" by Wang Chick in 868 AD. Some copies of the Buddhist scriptures printed in 1377 are preserved in museums in China. Though the Egyptians made paper by 3500 BC, it came to Europe only by the 11th century.

The period of 7th to 13th century can be regarded in the history of the printing of books as the age or religious "illuminated manuscript" production. Writing, copying, and illuminating were the popular techniques for producing books. During this period, books were made by hands and great pain was taken to decorate them. These books were largely of the religious types and their production was considered an act of worship. Scribes (or copiers) produced these books mainly in the monasteries that were spread across Europe. Monastic scribes wrote Bibles taking generally years for their production. They used to engrave each page on a block of wood using both pictures as well as the text as per the need. However, their main concentration used to be on the 'decoration' of the book in order to pay tribute to the word of God by conveying the beauty of God's message to mankind. By the method of engraving, they prepared numerous books. Interestingly, playing cards were also produced similarly by a set of blocks.

In the 12th and by the end of the 13th century, various universities (including Oxford and Cambridge) came into existence and a need of non – religious books was felt which could be easily available to the students. So, 13th to 15th centuries can be regarded as the age of "secularization" of book production. This proved to be revolutionary for the advent of a printing press since copying could not meet the demands of that day.

Europe did not witness these developments until the 15th century. The printing technology swept over Europe in 1400s. Johann Gutenberg a goldsmith by profession from the mining town of Mainz in Southern Germany, is generally credited with the invention of printing by movable type in the middle part of the 15th century. He, with his associates Fust and Schoeffer, got success in 1455 in mass printing of books by printing the first Latin Bible, called the Mazarin. He printed about 300 two volume Gutenberg Bibles which were sold at 30 florins per copy at that time. He developed his printing press by combining various technologies, viz. textile, wine presses, and papermaking.

From Germany, printing spread throughout Europe rapidly and in England also, where William Caxton established the first printing press in 1476. It was in 1530s that the first printing press in America was established in Mexico City, and the first such press was set up in South America is 1584 in Lima, Peru.

It is almost at this time that the first printing press was brought in India almost by accident on September 06, 1556 (Moses and Maslog, 1978). Actually the press was to be established in Ethiopia for the Christian missionaries. But the sudden death of the Jesuit priest who was accompanying the press led to the press remaining in India. This way, printing was introduced in India accidentally. After 22 years, in 1578, the second printing press was established by the Christian missionaries at a village – Punikael in Thirunelveli district of Tamil Nadu mainly to print religious books. The first non – missionary printing press – and the third in India – was established in Bombay in 1674.

However, it took 224 years to print the first newspaper in India since the first printing press came here (in 1559). The Bengal Gazette – first newspaper – came out on January 29, 1780. Printing in Hindi language appeared rather late and the first Hindi paper in 1826. This was just the beginning. After that many more presses were established and are being established. Enormous number of books and newspapers are being published each day in India alone.

Technology undergoes constant improvements and change. A number of improvements in the printing technology over the past few centuries have made it more efficient and effective. Nowadays, publishing a book has become easier and cheaper than before. The advent of computer technology has also revolutionized printing. Now, a large database can be easily stored in hard disks, floppy disks, compact disks, etc. Writers have gained unmatched freedom to prepare the manuscript in bits and pieces that can be assembled in any desired sequence within no time. By cutting and pasting procedure, words, sentences, and paragraphs can be shifted from one port of the text to another at no cost and in no time. One now does not need to bother much about spelling mistakes. By attaching printers to the computer, even children today can take print outs of the text. In sum, these new technologies and devices have not only improved the quality and accuracy of the printed text but have also made the process simpler and faster.

Q6. Discuss the relevance of print medium and distance education.

Or

What are the merits and demerits of print medium?

Ans. Print is the most accessible educational medium to most DE students. Most DE institutions still use print materials extensively as the main instructional medium, and many use print material to deliver 100 per cent of their course content. This is due to print's flexibility and accessibility. As Rowntree (1994a, b) have indicated, DE print materials must be carefully developed and/or adapted to meet the curriculum's specific goals and objectives. Various types of print material can be used: new materials produced by the institution, textbooks produced by other publishers and combinations of both (Lockwood, 1994). Previously produced textbooks may need explanation and adjustments to make them suitable as self-instructional DE materials, and so will need to be packaged with accompanying materials (articles, blueprints, guideline manuals, etc.). The DE institution will need to take care of the copyright aspects of using previously published instructional materials.

Merits of Print Medium: Print medium has certain merits that explain the reasons of its being universally useful in all modes of instruction including the distance education system. The merits of print medium are as follows:

(1) Cost – effective: It is less costly compared to other media.

(2) Easily editable, revisable and referable: As compared to sophisticated electronic devices and software, printed material is easy and cost – effective to edit and revise.

(3) Easy to use: The print material allows one to read at one's own pace and style (full or part, etc.).

(4) Portable: Books, magazines, etc. can be carried along and can be used anytime and anywhere. There is no rigidity of time – schedules like the one that goes with TV and radio programmes.

Demerits of Print Medium: The print medium suffers from some limitations. A few of these are:

(1) Time – consuming: Reading material consumes more time that viewing the same things through images, e.g. a TV programme.

(2) Not suitable to the needs of diverse learners: Often, the printed material is prepared keeping in mind the average readers/learners. Once printed, it does not change as per the needs of weak students or students with learning disabilities.

(3) Reading ability: Literacy and the knowledge of the language of printed material is an important factor.

(4) Unsuited for developing practical skills: Reading a printed lesson on how to drive a car is good to provide theoretical knowledge but it can hardly develop any such practical skills.

(5) Intelligence level: Readers are also required to possess adequate cognitive skills to comprehend the printed message.

In selecting an appropriate textbook for a course, two factors can be considered: its content (that is, relevance and scope in relation to the course topics); and non-content issues such as its appearance, reputation, availability and price. Guideline materials should be designed to be compatible with the textbook and should include details about:

- the course objectives;
- the relevance of the textbook's topics to the course objectives;
- the stages through which the course and the student's use of the materials will develop;
- exercises, case studies, simulations and other activities, as appropriate.

Q7. What do you mean by Self-learning materials? Discuss the nature of self-instructional materials.

Ans. Self-instructional materials refer to constituting of that type of learning materials and conditions which are arranged in that manner so that students can proceed to learn on their own with little or no supervision.

Traditional classroom environment has its own advantages and the field of distance education is widening its scope. It is not only economic than traditional education system but also caters the need of masses.

Hence more and more countries are opting this mode of teaching-learning.

In distance education, students are provided with printed lessons and/or audio-visual programmes, these learning materials are self-instructional materials and they have replaced a classroom teacher.

Nature of self-instructional materials: The nature of SIM depends upon the major style of learning which are as follows:

- Independently (without someone's help)
- Interdependently (with someone's help and cooperation).

The learners are motivated for ***independent learning*** or ***self-learning.*** Independent study or learning refers to, for the most part, the learning that is independent of teachers and institutions. This approach to approach to learning is the key element of distance education and learning.

(1) Independent or Self-Oriented Learners have following nature; found:

- enjoying learning by self,
- open to criticism and feedback,
- taking control of personal learning,
- enjoying finding solutions to the problems, etc.
- evaluating their learning progress and pace,
- to be self-reliant in collecting relevant information,
- finding enough time for learning,
- setting learning goals as per personal capabilities,
- preferring structured personal learning.

(2) On the other hand, the Other Oriented or Interdependent Learners are frequently found:

- asking others for help, guidance, and direction,
- preferring learning when with others and/or peers,
- searching for help in solving their learning problems, etc.
- depending on a facilitator for structuring learning activities,
- participating comfortably in group learning activities, and
- enjoying the support provided by a facilitator in learning,
- to be sensitive to criticism and feedback,

- requiring others for setting their learning goals,

Q8. Describe the characteristics of self-instructional materials.

Ans. As a teacher, trainer, and line manager or as a learner everyone must have used self-instructional material in open, distance or flexible learning contexts. In primary school it may have involved you giving children a work card in arithmetic to complete, a tactile puzzle to solve or directions to follow in playing a game. In secondary school you may have provided directions to conduct an experiment, data to solve a problem or guidelines to undertake project work. In further education & training you may have prepared materials to stimulate fault diagnosis or used multimedia & computer based packages to provide a resource for your teaching. At its simplest you may have given learners a technical report, blueprint, circuit diagram or extract to study together with a series of questions to answer. You may have followed the manufacturers instructions to assemble DIY furniture, programme the time control on the central heating or cooker-with different degrees of success! All of the above could constitute self-instructional material.

If you were involved in producing self-instructional material it would be worth considering what features of these materials you currently exploit plan. If you are planning to be involved you could consider what feature you could incorporate and thus maximize the effectiveness of your teaching.

Characteristics of self instructional material are as follows: The self-learning materials are designed based on learning theories, to a large extent on the basis of an eclectic approach combining behaviouristic, cognitive, and constructivist learning theories. Without going into these theories, we list five characteristics of self-learning materials: self-explanatory, self-contained, self-directed, self-motivating, and self-evaluating.

- **Self-Explanatory:** The self-learning materials are written in a way that does not require any intermediary (teacher) to explain the content. This means, the content is written in simple language and in small chunks to help distance learners assimilate the content by reading and working through the instructions. Thus, a teacher is built in, into the text. But, these are different from instructional manuals that come with electronic gadgets or home appliances.

- **Self-Contained:** The self-learning materials are prepared in such a way that the distance learners normally do not require additional materials to learn the concepts/ subject matter. This is highly important for the distance learners, since they are isolated and dispersed; they may not have access to good libraries and learning resources. Therefore, it is necessary that the learning materials supplied to them are detailed and self-contained in nature. This is also related to the nature of the 'curriculum' in distance education, which is open, whereas in face-to-face education, the curriculum is hidden in the syllabus. An open curriculum envisages that the content is clearly detailed, leaving nothing to the imagination of the learner and interpretation. Also, if a course requires the use of external source materials, these are supplied along with the course. For example, if a course requires the student to listen to an audio cassette then it should be supplied in the course pack to make it self-contained.
- **Self-Directed:** As distance learners study in isolation, it is important that the self-learning materials are designed in a way that provides necessary directions to the learners to study and progress. This is done in the self-learning materials by using a variety of techniques including the use of hints, notes, graphics (icons) and explicit directions on how to do, what to do and what is expected of the learner. The use of learning objectives, guidance in introduction, and a conversational style of writing text, instructions to do and how to answer the self-assessment questions are elements of self-direction that are used in self-learning materials to facilitate learning.
- **Self-Motivating:** One of the major roles of a teacher in the face-to-face education system is to motivate and encourage the learners towards study and research. Teachers are role models and students generally try to emulate their teachers. They create interest and curiosity towards a subject. In distance learning materials, all these features should be included, and good self-learning material should arouse curiosity, and interest, encourage the learners towards in-depth study and critical thinking, motivate them to question and reflect on their

own experiences and practices, and also provide reinforcement on learning progress. These are provided through the use of a personalized style of writing, use of anecdotes, examples, illustrations from real-life, feedback on self-assessment questions, etc.

- **Self-Evaluating:** It is important for the distance learners to know how they are progressing in their studies, particularly because they are quasi-permanently separated from the teachers and others in their peer group. The separation of teachers and learners inhibits two-way communication, and the learners may not get timely feedback or can't even compare their performance with other peer group members. Thus, the self-learning materials should provide self-assessment questions and their personalized feedback to allow the students to evaluate themselves and learn from their action (correct/ incorrect). The self-evaluating characteristics of distance learning materials envisage that the distance learners use the learning material in an active manner. Learning activeness is the key, where use of in-text questions, self-assessment questions, unit-end exercises, reflective action-based activities and feedback all play significant roles. The use of learning objectives in behavioural action verbs to measure the achievement of learning is also another way to empower the learner.

Besides these, there are some more characteristics of SLMs such as:

- The SLMs have clearly specified objectives.
- The content is learner-friendly, with the use of first and second person (I, You, etc.) in writing
- Consist of short and manageable chunks of contents for better understanding and learning.
- "A picture is worth a 1000 words". So, good SLMs should include pictures and illustrations (like tables, charts and graphs) to support and supplement the text, wherever required.
- Headings make the presentation systematic and highlight the major points which then become easy to comprehend.

Q9. Define access devices. Describe the relation of access devices with activities.

Or

What are the types of activities? Write the importance of activities.

Or

What are the precautions should be taken while designing activities?

Or

What do you mean by access devices? Discuss educational implications of different types of access devices used in self-learning materials.

Ans. According to the 'Glossary of terms commonly used in Distance Education' (STRIDE, IGNOU, 1997): Access devices are the devices used in self-instructional materials to help the learners locate concepts and ideas in any part of the material. They make the contents of learning text more accessible. Examples of access devices are: structure, objectives, advance organizers (information presented before learning and is used by the learner to organize and interpret the information later presented), content map, summary, glossary, etc.

These access devices perform the following three major functions:

- They help learners in finding what they are looking for in the text i.e. it offers a simple form of navigation.
- They present the material in more easy, understandable and highlighted form.
- They build the teacher into the course material.

Access devices are of different types. Global access devices present the overview of the text as a whole. It consists mainly of the aims and objectives, summary, index, and glossary. On the other hand, local access devices are those which label and highlight various parts of the text, for example headings and sub headings.

Assess devices are also divided into three types on the basis of their actual location in the content. A brief description of these is as follows:

- **Beginning of a Unit:** This portion consists of those access devices which appear before the actual presentation of the course content. It comprises the title, list of content/structure, objectives, introduction, etc.

- **Main Body:** Those access devices which appear at the main body of the course material. It includes introduction, headings and sub-headings, check your progress, summary, etc.
- **End part:** Access devices which appear after the main body of the course contents and mainly consists of a glossary of the terms used in the text, suggested further readings, answers to various self assessment exercises, unit-end-tests or assignments, references,

In the distance learning mode, SLM plays the role of the teacher. Hence, just as a teacher asks learners to perform certain activities during the course of teaching, similarly, the SLM too includes certain activities to ensure that learning is active and meaningful. Activities are a means of interacting with the learners and often help the learners to gain first hand experience.

There can be a wide range of activities like:

- applying learning to new and practical problems.
- suggesting new solutions to different issues and problems.
- expressing views on various subject matters.
- identifying, developing and demonstrating new skills.
- recalling learned course contents.
- drawing a table, graph, chart, etc.
- judging and evaluating fresh ideas.
- comparing new ideas with the old ones.

Types of Activities: STRIDE (IGNOU) has prepared taxonomy of activities which is as follows:

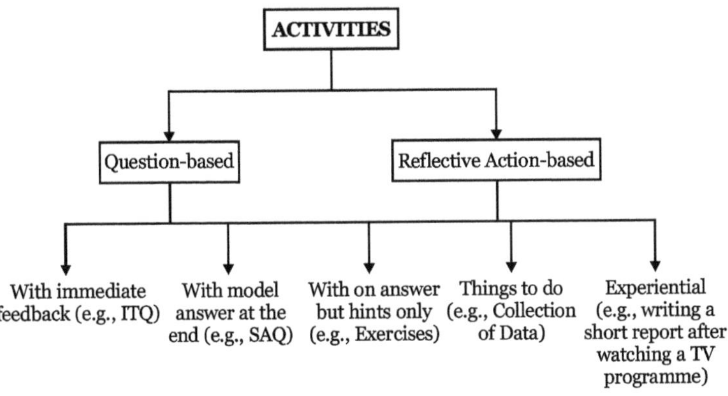

Let us have a brief look at some of the major types. We have just gone through the definition of activities. The first type of activity includes ***"question-based activities"***, requiring the learners to respond to the questions asked in the SLMs. These are further divided into three types. Can you notice any difference among these three types discussed above? Yes, it is regarding the delivery of feedback.

(1) In-Text Questions (ITQs): These are questions and activities embedded in the text itself. They help test learner's understanding of text. The basic purpose of this type of activity is to continuously interact with the learners through these questions. It keeps the interest and motivation of the learners alive because they are provided with the immediate feedback about these answers.

(2) Self-Assessment Questions (SAQs): These are aids for the learner to check his/her progress in studies and can be of a variety of types. You might have noticed that in order to give these a distinctive look, these are mostly put inside a plain box or sometimes within lines. The major purpose of these SAQs, once again, is to make the learners aware of their learning progress. You yourself might have gone through various types of SAQs given in your SLMs. The popular SAQs used by course authors are as follows:

True-false Items: These are the simplest types of SAQs. However, true-false items are criticised on various grounds like, as they are directly from the text, they encourage rote memorization. Secondly, they are simple and hence they cannot assess as per the complex instructional objectives. Moreover, they permit guesswork. Following is an example of True-False format:

Classify the following statements as true (T) or false (F). Write T or F in the boxes provided on the right hand side.

- Learning is a permanent change in behaviour.
- Good SLMs comprise a number of interactive devices, known as activities.
- Electronic media proves to be cheaper than print medium.
- Activities help one to apply learning to do the practical problems.

Multiple-Choice Items: As the name implies, many response alternatives to a single question are given. But only one response is correct and remaining incorrect response options act as ***distracters.*** The examinees are required to find out/identify the correct one.

You might note that finding out a correct response among many requires a good discriminating power and not only the ability to recall and recognize the correct option. Since you see many options, you cannot simply guess blindly as you could in the case of true-false type items. Also, an analysis of selected distracters might be required.

However, it is difficult to construct good multiple-choice items which contain equally attractive distracters to minimize the guessing. Secondly, recognition ability rather than recall and/or organization of information helps in answering theses questions. One can *recognize* the correct answer. Following is an example of Multiple-Choice Items:

Which among the following is ***not*** the characteristic of SLMs? Check the correct answer.

- Self-directed
- Self-motivating
- Self-esteem
- Self-evaluating

Matching Items: In this type of activity, a set of responses is to be matched to a set of options or premises. The basic distinction between true-false and multiple-choice items with this type is that the former has only one stimulus question and two or more response options. On the other hand, in this type there are multiple stimulus questions and multiple response options in the matching items. Here the learners is required to find out which response option matches with which stimulus option. Following is an example of Matching Items:

Match the items given in Column 1 with those in Column 2.

Column 1	**Column 2**
Technology	Scientific study of living things
Psychology	Scientific study of behaviour
Biology	Science put to useful practice

Short-Answer Type Items: As the name implies, these items require you to reply briefly. This category further contains three types of activities: (i) *fill in the blanks,* (ii) *sentence-completion items,* and (iii) *description tests.* 'Fill in the blanks' essentially is a recall type of activity as the learners are provided blanks within the sentences and are asked to fill in these blanks with suitable words. Sentence completion activities require learners to complete a half written sentence. Following is an example of Short-Answer Type Items:

(1) Fill in the blanks choosing the alternatives given within brackets:

(i) Learning is a relatively permanent change in ________. (thinking/feeling/nature/behaviour)

(2) Complete the following statements:

(i) Self-Learning is a process in which the learner __________.

(ii) The SLMs are an instrument of learning, and are different from _.

(3) Descriptive type SAQs: Define the following concepts in your own words (30-50) with the help of suitable examples:

(i) Classical Conditioning

(ii) Meaningful Learning

Importance of Activities: Activities are highly important for the following reasons:

- Activities provide an order and structure to the SLMs.
- Activities guide and check whether a learner is fulfilling the objectives.
- Activities not only generate interest and enthusiasm but also motivate for self-learning.

Precautions to be taken while designing Activities: Suppose, you are a course developer, in order to help the learners get maximum benefit from the activities, you need to consider the following points:

- identifying key areas in which the activities are to be developed.
- keeping in mind the nature of objectives while designing the activities.
- activities should be directly related and relevant to learners'. immediate needs and environment.
- the purpose of your activities should be clear to the learner.
- activity should match the learned course material.
- useful feedback - relevant to each activity should be provided.

Q10. Describe the procedure of development of self-learning print materials.

Ans. Parts of SLM discussed below should be developed in described manner:

(1) Initial Part of the Unit: From this heading, you rightly guessed that this is very first part of the unit which basically orients you to the unit. You will not find, however, this very heading in your SLM. This first part is dissected into the following three parts which you generally find in your course unit: Structure, Objectives and Introduction.

Structure of the Unit: Although most authors, as you usually see in the books and journals, name it as contents, in the distance education field, the term **structure** is preferred and used because of its pedagogical value. Under this heading, in your SLMs, you find detailed itemization of the content, which is divided into sections and sub sections as and if required. Here the structure serves the same basic purpose as an index in a book. In other words it is meant to guide you "where" you can find "what" easily. You may now take a close look at the 'structure' of the present unit.

Objectives of the Unit: This is a unique feature of the SLMs and rarely found in any text book. In simple words, an objective refers to a statement regarding some desired outcome. It specifies what a learner should be able to do or tell after going through a specific section. It is important to note that only the objective formation is not sufficient rather a constant check is also required to determine whether these objectives are achieved or not. Also, the use of verbs in 'stating your objectives in behavioural terms' is very crucial and essential. You might use verbs like define, explain, write, describe, state, outline, illustrate, identify, etc.

Introduction of the Unit: Under this heading, you are supposed to briefly introduce your unit. Here, along with emphasizing and linking the past knowledge of the learners, you should discuss the structure of the unit to explain what you are going to present in the unit. The basic theme of the unit is also to be given due importance. Besides, if available, you should mention special audio-visual aids, references, supplementary material which could help the learners for additional learning side by side. These are regarded as additional sources of help.

(2) Middle Part of the Unit: Now it is time to present your course content in the form of SLM in order to fulfill the objectives you set for your unit. It is better to divide your material in the form of short, manageable chunks which should be put under a section. Each section should be provided a unique and relevant heading, and should deal with on objective of your unit. Your content should be logically arranged and bound in a sequence to facilitate the learning. If the unit lacks logical arrangement and sequence of the content, the resulting jerks and ups and downs might cause the loss of interest and motivation in learning.

Furthermore, to give a personal touch, use of first and second person in writing SLM is recommended and preferred. So, it should seem like a conversation between the distant teacher and distant learner. Also, you should be very particular and careful in using the language in your unit. Simple and short sentences should be used, and passive voice and impersonal usages should not be used much. Also, simple, directly related and self-explanatory 'illustration' add to the effectiveness of a unit.

Up to now, you have been concerned with fulfilling your course objectives through sections and sub-sections of SLMs.

(3) End Part of the Unit: This section also is equally important as the previous two parts are. This end part consists of summary, glossary, references and suggested further readings, and model answers or clues to the unit activities and questions (e.g., SAQs). After you have discussed your material in sufficient details, you should revise and summarise your important points. This serves as feedback and promotes self-learning. Glossary has its own importance in the SLMs. Although it is not a compulsory part but should be provided if your content included some new concepts, terminology and words which require sufficient elaboration for full understanding. Further, many readers wish to read additional materials. In order to help them for additional learning, you should provide a list of useful reference and should suggest further readings which are easily available. Lastly, you should provide model answers or clues to the SAQs.

The following steps are generally followed for developing SIM:

Step I	Identify the target,
Step II	Identify the learning needs,
Step III	Decide the terminal behaviour,
Step IV	Identify the entry behaviour,
Step V	Develop the blueprint of the SIM. This speci? es (i) content outline, (ii) types of learning activities, (iii) types of learning aids, (iv) learning steps to be followed, (v) Evaluation step for each part of SIM, (vi) blueprint should be reviewed for further improvement,
Step VI	Develop SIM on the basis of an improved blueprint,
Step VII	Undertake a review to improve the SIM,
Step VIII	Try out the SIM on a limited scale,
Step IX	Evaluate the SIM in terms of learning process and learning outcomes
Step X	Improve the SIM based upon the feedback,

Q11. What is development testing? Write the ways by development testing can be done.

Ans. Do you know 'why food is a tasted in kitchen itself before serving it?' Yes, you are right. This ensures the quality of the food to be delivered. Same is to be followed here. After you have prepared the SLM you must conduct a **try-out** before submitting in for bulk printing. The process of ensuring quality of SLM is known as developmental testing. Developmental testing can be done in following two ways:

- **Face to Face Try-out:** Find out a few (4 - 5) sample learners from the target population for whom you are developing your SLM. Clarify your aim and intentions. Provide them with your unit and ask them to pinpoint your weak and difficult areas. Encourage and welcome comments, criticisms and suggestions. Note their points. Ensure that their responses are not affected by your presence. Wherever you feel it genuine, objectively modify your material. Is it not a cost-effective method for improving the quality of your SLM?
- **Field Trial:** In comparison to face to face try-out, this method takes much time and requires more systematic efforts in serving your purpose of improving the quality of your self-

learning materials. Here, you should have a sample of atleast 25-30 learners from the target population, experts, and experienced colleagues. Explain your purpose and ensure their cooperation. Send a copy of your unit to all of them with a request to critically evaluate this unit and detect difficult areas. For this purpose, you can also prepare a questionnaire in which the respondents might be asked to rate the effectiveness of various parts, sections and sub sections, activities, etc. of your SLM.

In your questionnaire, you may cover the following areas for developmental testing among others:

- Relevance and clarity of the objectives;
- Relevance and clarity of the contents;
- Relationship between theory and practics;
- Appropriateness of language;
- Usefulness of activities and feedback;
- Is the material capable of motivation of learners for self-learning?
- Are tables, charts, examples appropriate and related to the theory?
- Overall presentation of the material;
- Others as applicable.

After you receive the required feedback, analyze and compile that information, and modify your SLM as and where required. This way, you can ensure the quality and effectiveness of your SLM through developmental testing.

Q12. What do you mean by skills? Discuss the nature and types of skills.

Ans. Skills refers to finely coordinated, complex motor acts that are the result of perceptual motor learning, such as handwriting, golf, or pottery. However, skill is also used to refer to parts of acts that are primarily intellectual, as those involved in comprehension or thinking.

Skills could be academic like reading, writing, studying, calculating, etc. There are also other type of skills such as musical skills, dancing, playing an instrument, playing a game, cooking, etc.

There are three major characteristics of a skill.

- response chains,
- eye-hand coordination, and
- the organisation of S-R (stimulus-response) chains into complex response patterns.

(1) Motor responses are a product of stimulus-response (S-R) association and may also involve cognitive processes like thinking, analyzing, etc. This can be demonstrated by Gagne's (1965) illustration of a car driver who intends to start a car. Gagne has minutely dissected this process: when you wish to start the engine of your car (S), you look carefully at the road (R), when you find the road clear (S), you test whether the car is in neutral gear (R), when you find the gear in neutral (S), you turn the key to activate the starter (R), and so on.... Note that your responses in this example are muscular movements which involve the use of eyes, arms, legs, fingers, etc.

(2) Eye-hand coordination: Skilled behaviour also consists of good coordination between hands and eye movements (Bilodeau and Bilodeau, 1961). For example, batting in the cricket game is such a behaviour that requires good perceptual-motor skills. Thirdly, skilled behaviour is the organisation and application of S-R chains into complex and larger response patterns. Piloting a plane, working on a computer, typewriting skills, etc. are good examples of it which require a number of discrete actions instead of some single unitary act.

One more pertinent issue regarding the study of skills which relates to the classification of the skills. Fitts (1962, 1964) classified the skills on the basis of constancy - i.e. uniformity found in the highly skilled behaviours. Constancies, which differ in their levels of complexity, can be conceived of in terms of the movements made by body during skill performance. Fitts (1962) suggests that, at the lowest level of complexity, the body is in the resting positing while you perform a skill like threading a needle. Here the external object is fixed in relation to which you perform some skilled behaviour. At a more complex level of constancy, you perform a skill when your body is in motion and the targets (external) objects are fixed as for example running to bowl in cricket; where initially the body is not in motion but is required to be in motion at a later stage. For example, a shooter might be required to shoot at a moving target. Lastly, at the most complex level, both the body as well as the external objects are in motion, as in polo game.

In addition to gross body movements, skilled behaviour can also be classified in terms of certain S-R chain properties like coherence, continuity, and complexity, Coherence of the chains refers to the degree of dependence of successive responses. Swimming is less coherent than playing some musical instrument. Continuity refers to the degree to which the skilled responses are continuous. Controlling and balancing the steering wheel of a car shows continuity whereas batting in the cricket game is a discrete task. Lastly, the complexity of the S-R chains is determined by the variety of different stimuli and responses possible at a given time. Hence, learning the Ludo game is less complex than chess.

Q13. What do you mean by reading? Discuss in brief.

Ans. "Reading" is the process of looking at a series of written symbols and getting meaning from them. When we read, we use our eyes to receive written symbols (letters, punctuation marks and spaces) and we use our brain to convert them into words, sentences and paragraphs that communicate something to us.

In reading is defined as an ability to decode text, a skill that can be acquired by the end of third grade, it follows that this performance objective is a rather teleological process based on mastery and rote skill–one in which students gain input from text without engaging in critical Stances. Such a unitary definition of reading, easily quantified through a precise list of cumulative skills, strategies, and behaviours, have long been critiqued for leading to a deficit view of children and their meaning-making abilities. However, this type of restricted definition also places students, especially those who struggle with school-sanctioned literacies, at a particular disadvantage in a world that is increasingly driven by digital technologies, media saturation, and worldwide marketplaces that rely upon economies of attention.

Q14. Define the theories of reading by Gibson and Levin (1975) and Resnick and Weaver (1979).

Ans. Gibson and Levin recommend that practice emphasize both the purpose of reading–deriving meaning from the written word–and the requirement for reading, the flexible use of all sources of information: phonological, graphemic, semantic, and syntactic. Although they recognize that some students and some subskills require more practice than others, Gibson and Levin argue that drill on separate subcomponents of the process serves to create a new problem: how to go about integrating component parts into a smoothly functioning skill. They propose a multilevel approach and suggest that specific subskills be practiced only within a meaningful context. In this way, special attention can be given to troublesome levels but always in relation to , and never separate from, other levels.

Although the type of practice advocated by Gibson and Levin (1975) may be appropriate for most children, for some, this approach could constitute an information overload. Perhaps the procedure could be modified somewhat for these children by locating small bits of information within a meaningful context. This would reduce the level of complexity and, at the same time, keep the purpose of reading in view. Very little is known about optimal conditions for practicing written language skills. Because practice is so essential to the development of any skill, this aspect of learning to read and to spell ought to be the subject of further investigation.

Resnick & Weaver (1979) provide a comprehensive examination of the issues associated with learning to read including: (1) significance of decoding, (2) the nature of reading skills, (3) the relationship between reading and language, (4) factors that interfere with learning to read, (5) and the acquisition of reading competence. The general model that emerges from many different analyses is that early stages of reading depend upon letter-sound correspondence with increasing importance upon semantic-linguistic aspects over time.

Q15. Discuss Barrett's Taxonomy of reading comprehension.

Ans. The Barrett taxonomy designed originally to assist classroom teachers in developing comprehension question and/or test questions for reading, is especially useful for classroom questioning in the content area as well. The term "taxonomy of reading" or "taxonomy of reading comprehension" means the same thing. The most widely accepted taxonomy is the Barrett's taxonomy of reading comprehension. Now, let us discuss Barrett's taxonomy in details. The four categories of Barrett's taxonomy are:

(1) Literal Comprehension or Literal Recognition (Recall): It emphasizes the recognition or recall of ideas, information and happenings that are clearly/vividly stated in the materials to be read. Literal comprehension consists of the following six crucial aspects:

(i) Recognition or Recall of comparisons: where the reader can identify the likeness and differences in the text.

(ii) Recognition or Recall of Sequence: where the reader can recognize or recall the order of events or actions in the text.

(iii) Recognition or Recall of Cause and Effect Relationship: where the reader can identify causes and consequences mentioned in the text.

(iv) Recognition or Recall of Character Traits; where the reader can highlight the traits of a character.

(v) Recognition or Recall of Details: where the reader can locate or identify or call up from memory the names of characters or a narration given in the text.

(vi) Recognition or Recall of Main Ideas: where the reader can identify a given idea in the text.

(2) Inferential Comprehension: Inferential Comprehension refers to the logical conclusion - drawn form statements through deduction or induction. This is demonstrated when a student successfully synthesizes the content of the selected reading matter. His/her personal knowledge, intuitions and imagination are the bases for conjectures or hypotheses formed after reading. The six steps of literal comprehension given above can be inferred besides inferring figurative languages and predicting outcomes.

(3) Evaluation: Evaluation refers to the judgments made by the reader about the content of their reading by comparing the same with external criteria like information provided by the teacher, or by experts or by renowned writers or by authentic sources on the world-wide-web on the subject. Evaluation tasks related to reading are judgments about reality or fantasy, facts or opinions, or appropriateness or worth, desirability and acceptability or appropriateness

(4) Appreciation: Appreciation involves the reader's awareness of the literary techniques, forms, styles and structures employed by the author to stimulate emotion. This requires varying degrees of inference and evaluation with the reader's sensitivity to appreciate the technique used by the author, as the task that involves appreciation are emotional responses to a plot or theme; identification with characters and incidents, reaction to the author's use of language; sensitivity towards imagery, etc.

Q16. Discuss the SQ3R system of improving reading skills.

Ans. Francis Robinson in 1961 put forth the SQ3R system (designated by the initials S-Q-R-R-R, standing for survey, question, read, recite, and review) after consciously incorporating several aspects of the learning theory. SQ3R system guides the reader to activate his background knowledge on the subject; formulate questions to stimulate curiosity and stay focused; participate in deep information processing necessary for comprehension and recall; monitor comprehension and test readiness.

(1) Survey: This refers to a quick browsing of the title page, preface, chapter headings and sub-headings, graphical aids, introduction, summary, conclusion, terms or phrases in italics, bold face print, end-of chapter questions. Thus 'survey' enables one to gather the information necessary to focus and formulate goals.

(2) Question: This task helps one to engage his/her mind and concentrate on the text. The questions raised directly affect the ease with which the text can be comprehended. Survey of the text leads to questions. The questions posed by the authors and the end-of-chapter questions also serve as a mean of effective reading.

(3) Read: This refers to active reading. Unless the reader reads 'actively' the questions which have been formulated s/he can never satisfactorily attain learning. So, it helps to fill in the information around the mental structures one has been building during the process of 'survey'. Reading the text is the first step in learning.

(4) Recite: Refers to recalling the content read them from memory. Recitation helps to get the things read retained. Frequent recall helps improve concentration, chance to remedy misinterpretation(s) and develop critical reading.

(5) Review: This is done through the four above mentioned steps i.e. survey, question, read and recite. Review helps to check the validity of recall confirms whether the passage has to be reread. Review enables to refine the organization and building of memory.

Q17. What is the meaning of study skills? Discuss the strategies for effective study skills.

Ans. Study skills can be referred to the strategies to be developed by a learner to derive the greatest possible benefit from activities like listening, speaking, reading, writing, or advance skills which are not purely mechanical but require active mental exercise on the part of the learner.

Study skills strategies are the commonly adapted methods to ensure effective studying. The main study skill strategies usually practiced by most learners are as follows:

(1) Note taking: Notes can be taken either during lectures or after reading a text. Such organized notes serve as a permanent record which helps learner to remember the major and important point easily. Some of the essential aspects of note taking are:

- Recording (the information, only relevant portions)
- Reducing (the information, only relevant portions)
- Reciting (recalling the information)
- Reflecting (on the information)

(2) Setting studying time: Set a fixed time to begin studying. It is found that certain behaviours are conditioned with certain times of the day, and are performed successfully if taken well care of the habituated time. Also, just before study time, do not start some other, time-consuming business.

(3) Quiet and disturbance-tree environment: Set a comfortable place for study and study only. It noise, music and people disturb you, avoid them, if possible. If not possible, habituate yourself to reading and studying in that environment, and you will find yourself able to concentrate these too.

(4) Preferably, set small and short-range goals for yourself: Dividing your text into subsections (or whole into parts) can do this. However you should prepare a ***flexible schedule*** in which you have some time for friends, family, and entertainment also.

(5) Reward yourself on achieving your goal: You may recall what you had read about operant conditioning in an earlier unit. Positive reinforcement ensures you the reoccurrence of the desired bebaviour in future. So, when you use your study time effectively, and achieve the goals successfully, reward your self with some time for entertainment (watching TV for some time, or talking to a friend). Use this time the way you like as a positive reinforcement.

Q18. Discuss about the learning from print materials. What are the implications for print material development?

Ans. The printed course materials, are self-learning in nature, simulating learner-teacher interaction. Furthermore, appropriate information and communication technologies are used to facilitate just-in-time contacts among distance learners and teachers. The delivery model also incorporates an instructional system that uses performance-based learning processes and this enables you to demonstrate your understanding of the content-areas. The intensive competence-based course format allows you to take more responsibility for your own learning. In order to cater to the varying learning styles, the Institute offers the subject material in the following modes:

- **Downloadable mode:** Downloadable mode empowers to offer education in a dynamic from to students. Students can assess lessons, assignments and submit their scripts online. They need brood if they miss lessons-they can download their lesson notes and access archived lessons, tutorial sessions, lectures, etc.
- **Read-only mode:** Students will be able to only read the course concepts, downloads or interactive sessions are unavailable.
- **Classroom interaction:** The interactive learning provides an environment for students to talk and discuss freely about any related topics on or off line.

The reading and study skills have both direct and indirect implications for print material development.

While developing the print material in order to optimize the reading and study skills of the learners, care should be taken to:

- Have differences in font size for the headings/sub headings and running text.
- use non-verbal aids such as the use of italics, bold letters, etc. amidst the running text so that the reader can grasp and interpret the content with care.
- provide summary at the end of the unit so that the crux of the chapter is available in a nutshell.
- furnish important points in boxes so that the reader can read and remind himself of the main point in that chapter.
- Leave wide margins at the left for notes.
- Include questions and activities that induce reflection.

World Wide Web: Loosely used, the WWW (or Web) refers to the whole constellation of resources that can be accessed using gopher, FTP, HTTP, Telnet, Usenet, WAIS, and other tools. The WWW is a hypertext-based, distributed information system originally created by researchers at CERN, the European Laboratory for Particle Physics, to facilitate sharing research information. The Web presents the user with documents, called web pages, full of links to other documents or information systems. Selecting one of these links, the user can access more information about a particular topic. Web pages include text as well as multimedia (images, video, animation, and sound). Servers are connected to the Internet to allow users to traverse, or surf, as it is called, the Web using a web browser.

Chapter-4

Audio and Video Media

Q1. Describe, briefly, the historical development of broadcast media.

Or

Discuss the history of broadcasting of radio and television in India.

Ans. History of Indian Radio is the history of radio broadcast that started in India with the setting up of a private radio service in Chennai, in the year 1924. In that same year, British government gave license to the Indian Broadcasting Company, to launch Radio stations in Mumbai and Kolkata. Later as the company became bankrupt, the government took possession of the transmitters and began its operations as the Indian State Broadcasting Corporation. In the year 1936, it was renamed All India Radio (AIR) and the Department of Communications managed it entirely. After independence, All India Radio was converted into a separate Department. All India Radio has five regional headquarters in New Delhi, for the North Zone; in Kolkata, for the East Zone; in Guwahati, for the North-East Zone, in Mumbai, for the West Zone; and in Chennai, for the South Zone.

In the year 1957, All India Radio was renamed Akashvani, which is controlled by the Ministry of Information and Broadcasting. During the period of independence only a mere 6 radio stations existed throughout the country. But during the late 1990s, the network of All India Radio extended to almost 146 AM stations. Moreover the Integrated North-East

Service focused on reaching to the population in northeast India. All India Radio offers programmes in English, Hindi and numerous regional and local languages. In the year 1967, Commercial Radio services started in India. The initiative was taken by Vividh Bharati and Commercial Service, from the headquarters in Mumbai. Vividh Bharati accumulated revenues from widespread sponsorships and advertisements. During the mid-1990s, broadcasting was carried on from 31 AM and FM stations.

By 1994, there were around 85 FM stations and 73 short wave stations that linked the whole nation. The broadcasting technology in India is basically indigenous and reaches far and wide to various listeners like farmers who require various updated information on agriculture. Between 1970 and 1994, the amount of radio receivers increased manifold, almost five times. From the initial 14 million, the number increased to a staggering 65 million. The broadcast services from foreign countries are provided by the External Services Division of All India Radio. Almost 70 hours of news, entertainment programmes were broadcasted in 1994 in various languages with the help of 32 shortwave transmitters.

After Independence, Indian radio was regarded as a vital medium of networking and communication, mainly because of the lack of any other mediums. All the major national affairs and social events were transmitted through radio. Indian radio played a significant role in social integration of the entire nation. All India Radio mainly focused on development of a national consciousness as well as over all National integration. Programming was organised and created keeping in mind the solitary purpose of national political integration. This supported in prevailing over the imperative crisis of political instability, which was created after the Independence. Thus political enhancement and progressive nation building efforts were aided by the transmission of planned broadcasts.

All India Radio also provided assistance in enhancing the economic condition of the country. Indian radio was particularly designed and programmed to provide support to the procedure of social improvement, which was a vital pre-requisite of economic enhancement. The leading development beliefs of the time analysed the problems and hindrances in development as the primary ones in the developing nations. The function of broadcasting paved a way for the surge of modern concepts. Later, with the modernisation of the country, television was introduced and broadcasting achieved new status. But by then, radio had become a veteran medium in India. Diverse programmes including entertainment and melodious songs were also transmitted nationwide. Akashvani or All India Radio still stands as one of the biggest radio networks around the globe.

Even though entertainment programmes form the bulk of day-to-day broadcasts and commanded maximum listenership, educational programmes have always been a compulsory factor in the fixed-point charts of all the radio stations. Usually you find a typical radio station airing school broadcasts, for schools, universities and distance education learners, which are broadcast from different AIR stations both on medium wave and short-wave. Since 1993, programmes meant for IGNOU student are being broadcast from select AIR stations regularly.

The National Education Policy document of 1986 and also the Programme of Action, 1992 underpinned the need for harnessing radio for educational purposes. The real breakthrough in this regard came in the year 1999, when the Ministry of Information and Broadcasting took a policy decision to throw open FM Radio to private broadcasters at 40 select places in the country. While unveiling the scheme, one frequency at each of the 40 places was kept reserved for educational broadcasting and passed them on to the Ministry of Human Resource Development for establishing the FM radio stations. The Indira Gandhi National Open University was chosen as the nodal agency to implement the project within a time frame of 3 years starting from the year 2001-02. These stations were established under the banner 'Gyan Vani': Allahabad, Banglore, Coimbatore, Lucknow, Mumbai, Vishakhapatnam and Bhopal. With daily transmission ranging from 8 hours to 12 hours and a coverage area of about 60 km radius each.

The Gyan Vani network of 26 stations aims to address the educational and development needs of the local communities. Each Gyan Vani station operates in an autonomous manner with the collaboration of local educational institutions and NGO's in the day-to-day management and running of the station. Live educational lessons with phone-in-interactions from the target audience are the noteworthy features of Gyan Vani broadcasts at all the places. The medium is usually English or Hindi or the local language. At present there is transmission of educational and enrichment audio programmes through FM Radio network of the Gyan Vani Stations located at different places of the country. There is also transmission of live Interactive Radio Counseling (IRC) sessions for IGNOU students through AIR Stations.

Television: Television came to India in September 1959 as an educational experiment involving- UNESCO. Doordarshan, the public TV network run by Prasar Bharti, has a monopoly of terrestrial broadcasting, with 67 studio centres and 1, 415 transmitters, and operates 35 channels: 7 national channels, 11 regional language satellite channels, 12 state networks, and 1 international channels. The flagship DDI channels reaches some 400 million viewers. In 2013, there were 795 private satelite TV channels a 17 percent CAGR (com-pounded annual growth rate) of the television industry during 2011-2016 (–Television: Social Television introduced in India in September 1959 as an educational experiment involving UNESCO. The transmission timings were just about 20 minutes, twice a week. School Television (STV) was started in 1961 and entertainment programmes in 1965, by which time daily transmission too were introduced.

The expansion of Indian television began in 1982-83: Doordarshan, the government's television organization, began to use Indian communication satellites to broadcast in color a new set of programmes, including the Asian Games of 1982 and the National Programme, sent from New Delhi to stations throughout India. In 1982 Doordarshan's 16 transmitters reaches less than 8 percent of Indian people, but in 1983 the Sixth Five-Year Plan committed 869.5 million rupees to increase transmission facilities. By 1991 Doordarshan had 523 transmitters broadcasting programmes to 35 million TV sets and with the potential to reach almost 80 percent of the population.

Even in rural India, almost 19 percent of house-holds owned a television by 2001.

In 1984 the University Grants Commission (UGC) telecasts (later called 'country wide classroom') were introduced. The second channel of Doordarshan from Delhi was also commenced that year. The VCR (Video Cassette Recorder) revolution too made its beginning in the 80's, and soon made inroads into the nooks and corners of the country. Theatrical viewing of feature films, which till then had been the most popular pastime of the masses, suffered a setback as the 'video boom' readily offered everyone the more convenient and cheaper alternatives of domestic viewing through VHS (Video Home System) cassettes.

The television scene in the 1990s was marked by initiatives like development of transnational TV channels through satellites and the spread of cable. The hitherto unchallenged dominance of Doordarshan gave way to dozens of foreign as well as domestic TV channels, which competed fiercely with one another for viewership and advertisement revenues. While most of these channels are entertainment-oriented, there are notable exceptions like the 'Discovery Channel' and the 'National Geographic' which are dedicated to exploration and adventure documentaries.

IGNOU telecasts on Doordarshan made a modest start in 1991 with half hour slots on alternate days. In due course, they were extended to all days of the week. A separate educational TV channel, 'Gyan Darshan' was started on 26th Jan, 2000. Gyandarshan is a satellite-based channel airing programmes contributed by major educational bodies in the country such as IGNOU, UGC-CEC, NCERT-CIET, National Institute of Open Schooling, etc. Another significant development is the birth of the technology channel 'Ekalavya' which started on 26th Jan, 2003, as part of the Gyan Darshan bouquet, to cater to engineering students. Gyan Darshan (GD), a fully digital 24 hours exclusive Educational TV Channel, is a digital bouquet of 4 channels.

Doordarshan, the public TV network run by Prasar Bharti, has a monopoly of terrestrial broadcasting, with 67 studio centres and 1, 415 transmitters, and operates 35 channels: 7 national channels, 11 regional language satellite channels, 12 state networks, and 1 international channel. The flagship DD1 channel reaches some 400 million viewers. In 2013, there were 795 private satelite TV channels in India. FICCI-KPMG (2012) estimates a 17 percent CAGR (compounded annual growth rate) of the television industry during 2011-2016

Q2. Describe major sub-systems of any radio broad casting system.

Ans. Broadcasting of radio consists of following sub-system:

(1) Studio: The studio center is the place where the programmes are recorded, edited, produced, and played back at the time of transmission. This is the place where all recordings, editing, dubbing, mixing, live broadcast and announcements during transmission take place. In the case of live broadcasts, the studio center again is the place of origin of the programmes with the concerned artists/performances/ announcer/news readers operating from one or the other studio of the studio center. Even in the case of OB's (outside broadcast), the events being broadcast from the OB spot are invariably routed through the studio center for convenience of switching and other technical reasons. Thus the studio center becomes the eventual outlet for the programmes in all cases.

A studio center may have just one or more studios designed for recording different kinds of programmes. These are as follows:

(i) Transmission Studio: This is for the purpose of playing back pre-recorded tapes interspersed by live announcements etc. in a pre-determined sequence. The number of transmission studios (also called playback studios) would depend upon the number of broadcast channels that the station handles. All India Radio's Broadcasting House (BH) in Delhi, for example, contains 36 studios – some of them for production, and the rest for transmission.

(ii) Multi-purpose Studio: Smaller production houses cannot afford to create separate studios for individual purposes like talks, drama, music, etc. In this case, a single multi-purpose studio is the answer. The acoustics of a multi-purpose studio can be designed essentially for talks. When it has to be used for music or drama, reverberation can be added electronically (such electronic devices are available and are common as a part of the control room set up) in the right magnitude.

(2) Control Room: Radio broadcasting sub-system included a control room which refers to the focal area at which all the technical activities in a studio center converge. Engineers in control room have overall responsibility for the technical operations in the studio set up, for switching of broadcast feeds to the transmitting center and incoming feeds from external sources. In particular, the following functions are carried out in the control room:

(i) To distribute the programmes to respective transmitters, other radio stations that may be forming a network for programme exchange, satellite up-link facility or to any other destination.

(ii) To receive programmes online from each studio (through the respective announcer booth), and from external, sources like the radio-networking terminal, outside broadcast spot, etc.

Thus, the control room set-up is primarily an electronic switching system. These switching operations are performed by using a 'control console'. The control console has provision for continuous monitoring of the ongoing programmes either through headphones or loudspeakers to control their audio levels. The audio levels are carefully controlled, as too high a level will cause distortion and also overload the transmitter. On the contrary, too low a level will cause poor signal-to-noise ratio and, ultimately, poor reception in the radio sets.

(3) Audio Mixer: Audio mixer is the generic term for the announcer console (a device for combining, routing, and changing the level, tone, and/or dynamics of audio signals. From an operational stand point, an audio mixer can be understood as an equipment to which all the sources in the audio and announcer booth (microphones, tape decks, CD player, etc) are connected and from which the selected source(s) at any time can be passed on to the succeeding stages of the broadcast chain, or for other purposes like monitoring, recording, editing etc. Like so many other electronic gadgetry, audio mixers too are available in a wide range of models, facilities and technical features.

A minimum of eight channels (eight different sources) can be kept connected to the mixer: say 3 or 4 microphone channels and the rest of tape deck, CD player, cassette player, etc. Bigger recording studios meant for western orchestra use many more microphones simultaneously and therefore the channel capacity of the mixer too needs to be larger in their case.

(4) Announcer Booth: An announcer booth is attached with each of the production studios. While the actual programme (talk/discussion/drama/music concert/etc.) takes place inside the studio, the Announce Booth serves various related works like keeping continuity with programmes from other studios, linking announcements, playing filler music and pre-recording material, playback of pre-recorded music into the studio, etc.

(5) Studio-to-Transmitter Link (STL): The programmes emanating from the studio center are transported electronically to the transmitting center through the STL. This is because, in most cases, broadcast transmitters are located several kilometers away from the studio center, usually in the outskirts of the city. This fact necessitates some form of electronic link between the studio and transmitter. In the few cases where a transmitter is co-located as they require a large area for the aerial field with the studio, this link can be a hard-wired connection between the two.

In practice, STL can be any one of the several technical options available as follows:

(i) **Coaxial Cable:** Coaxial cable connection is generally more robust than a telephone line in its physical construction and performances. Coaxial cables are relatively less prone to loss during signal transmission and protect the signals from cross-talk and other interferences. For longer STL routes, coaxial cables are preferred over telephone lines.

(ii) **Microwave Link, FM Radio & Satellite:** Microwave, FM radio and satellite links offer wireless solutions for STL. In all these cases the transmitting equipment (Microwave transmitter/FM transmitter/satellite uplink) is installed as part of the studio center and corresponding receiving system at the radio transmitter site.

(iii) **Telephonic Lines:** Dedicated leased telephone lines are the most popular form of STL. Normal telephone lines have a narrow frequency response which is good enough for telephonic conversation but not as a transparent medium for broadcast quality audio. Hence the telephone lines used for STL are specially 'loaded' for improved frequency response and carefully maintained to prevent breakdown or loss of quality.

(6) Transmitting Center: The transmitting center it the place which house the radio transmitter and the antenna system with the help of which the programmes are transformed into 'radio' frequencies and radiated in the form of 'electromagnetic' waves. A separate radio transmitter is needed for each broadcast channel. In the case of a radio station broadcasting many channels, the transmitting center houses that many individual transmitters and contains an elaborate technical infrastructure and a sprawling aerial field, with masts of different heights and shapes towering over the surrounding landscape.

In the case of radio stations broadcasting multiple channels, (say, Delhi 'A', Delhi 'B', etc.) the transmitting center may house all the concerned transmitters (and the antennas) in the same place.

Alternatively, a transmitting center may contain just one transmitter, to cater to a single-channel station. In either case, a separate transmitter with a distinct 'carrier frequency' is essential for each broadcast channel.

For example, Delhi 'A' channel is broadcast through a transmitter which operates at a carrier frequency of 809 Hz (medium wave), while Delhi 'B' is broadcast through another transmitter operating at a carrier frequency of 1020 KHz (again in the medium wave).

(7) Radio Receivers: The universal popularity of radio broadcasting particularly in the rural and remote areas is mainly on account of its simple reception mechanism- the radio set.

Irrespective of the type or model, all radio sets receive the broadcasts in the same way: the basic receptor is the receiving aerial. Communication receivers use externally installed aerials of different shapes and lengths especially for HF reception (i.e. SW Band). In all other receiver sets, it is the in-built telescopic rod aerial whose length and orientation are adjustable for best reception of the particular HF broadcast. MW Broadcast are picked up by a ferrite rode aerial mounted inside the set. For best reception, the orientation of this has to be adjusted in the horizontal plane and, for this purpose, the set itself will have to be rotated.

(8) Microphones: The primary source of audio in any broadcast studio is the microphone. It is an indispensable device for audio recording, whether inside the studio or outside. At this stage the following particular may be noted for a preliminary understanding of the subject. Microphone (mike for short) is a device which converts sounds into electrical signals. These electrical signals are further amplified and processed in succeeding stages of the broadcast chain. These are different kinds of microphones to suit different occassions places and purposes. From a programmer's standpoint, there are two broad categories or microphones:

(i) Uni-directional microphones: There are mikes which can pick up sounds very well only in one direction and hardly from other directions. In other words, uni-directional mikes are like a sensitive ear in the direction in which they are pointed, whereas they are deaf to sounds coming from all other directions. These mikes are much more sensitive than omni-directional ones in the particular direction in which they are pointed; so they can be used to pick up of sounds from a distance e.g. in outdoor locations for sports events. In the studios, unidirectional mikes can be used for announcers/news reader and in radio plays.

(ii) **Omni-directional microphone:** These are mikes which can pick up sounds from any direction equally well. When such a mike is placed at the center of a table with the persons seated all around, all the voices will be picked up by it without any discrimination. In studios, omni-directional mikes can be used for group discussions and multi-way interviews, as a single mike would suffice the purpose and provides operational convenience.

Q3. Differentiate between AM and FM Radio Waves.

Ans.

	AM	**FM**
Stands for	AM stands for Amplitude Modulation	FM stands for Frequency Modulation
Origin	AM method of audio transmission was first successfully carried out in the mid 1870s.	FM radio was developed in the United states in the 1930s, mainly by Edwin Armstrong.
Modulating differences	In AM, a radio wave known as the "carrier" or "carrier wave" is modulated in amplitude by the signal that is to be transmitted. The frequency and phase remain the same.	In FM, a radio wave known as the "carrier" or "carrier wave" is modulated in frequency by the signal that is to be transmitted. The amplitude and phase remain the same.
Pros and cons	AM has poorer sound quality compared with FM, but is cheaper and can be transmitted over long distances. It has a lower bandwidth so it can have more stations available in any frequency range.	FM is less prone to interference than AM. However, FM signals are impacted by physical barriers. FM has better sound quality due to higher bandwidth.
Frequency Range	AM radio ranges from 535 to 1705 KHz (OR) Up to 1200 bits per second.	FM radio ranges in a higher spectrum from 88 to 108 MHz. (OR) 1200 to 2400 bits per second.
Bandwidth Requirements	Twice the highest modulating frequency. In AM radio	Twice the sum of the modulating signal frequency

	broadcasting, the modulating signal has bandwidth of 15kHz, and hence the bandwidth of an amplitude-modulated signal is 30kHz.	and the frequency deviation. If the frequency deviation is 75kHz and the modulating signal frequency is 15kHz, the bandwidth required is 180kHz.
Zero crossing in modulated signal	Equidistant	Not equidistant
Complexity	Transmitter and receiver are simple but syncronization is needed in case of SSBSC AM carrier.	Tranmitter and reciver are more complex as variation of modulating signal has to beconverted and detected from corresponding variation in frequencies.(i.e. voltage to frequency and frequency to voltage conversion has to be done).
Noise	AM is more susceptible to noise because noise affects amplitude, which is where information is "stored" in an AM signal.	FM is less susceptible to noise because information in an FM signal is transmitted through varying the frequency, and not the amplitude.

Q4. What do you mean by Ham Radio?

Ans. Amateur Radio or "ham radio" is one of the longest-lived wireless activities. Amateur experimenters were operating right along with Marconi in the early part of the 20th century. They have helped advance the state-of-the-art in radio, television and dozens of other communications services since then, right up to the present day. There are more than half a million amateur radio operators or "hams" in the United States alond and several million more around the world!

Amateur radio (also called "ham" radio) is the use of designated radio frequency spectra for purposes of private recreation, non-commercial exchange of messages, wireless experimentation, self-training, and emergency communication. The term "amateur" is used to specify "a duly authorised person interested in radioelectric practice with a purely personal aim and without pecuniary interest (either direct monetary or other similar reward) and to differentiate it from commercial broadcasting, public safety (such as police and fire), or professional two-way radio services (such as maritime, aviation, taxis, etc.).

The amateur radio service (amateur service and amateur satellite service) is established by the International Telecommunication Union (ITU) through the International Telecommunication Regulations. National governments regulate technical and operational characteristics of transmissions and issue individual stations licenses with an identifying call sign. Prospective amateur operators are tested for their understanding of key concepts in electronics and the host government's radio regulations. Radio amateurs use a variety of voice, text, image, and data communications modes and have access to frequency allocations throughout the RF spectrum to enable communication across a city, region, country, continent, the world, or even into space.

Q5. How television works?

Ans. The basic device that converts the real world scenes into TV signals is the video camera. A process called 'scanning' that takes place inside the camera does this. The light from the real world scene enters the video camera through its lens system in the front and converges insides the camera, where it forms a tiny optical image of the real scene. This optical image is a true replica of the real world scene- with all its detail, the motion and colours exactly reproduced therein. A beam of electrons inside the camera 'scans' this optical image point-by-point, line-by-line, and from top to bottom, much as we read the page of this unit: each line word-by-word, and from top to bottom, as we go along. As it scans, the optical information contained at each point (brightness and colour) is translated as a 'video signal'.

When the electron beam comes to the last point at the bottom of the optical image (in other words, when the scanning of the image is completed), the electronic system in the camera makes the beam to quickly bounce back to the top of repeat the process of scanning all over again. Technically, one cycle of scanning is called a 'frame' and the process takes place so rapidly that as many as 25 frames are scanned with just one second.

The video signals thus generated go through a complex chain of equipment, get transmitted and finally reach your TV set. Inside the TV set, the same process of scanning takes place in exact synchronization with the one inside the camera. The electron beam in the picture tube (that is, TV screen) 'writes' the image point-by-point and line-by-line, thereby recreating the total optical image, as it was formed inside the camera. In other words, the TV system generates discreet still images of the real scene from instant, but they are generated at a rapid rate of 25 frames per second. The human eye suffers from a limitation called 'Persistence of Vision' (in this context, it is to be seen as an advantage), because of which it cannot distinguish such rapid changes: instead, it perceives the image as a single one with motion contained in it. This property, coupled with the fact that TV signals travel as fast as light, makes the television broadcasting possible.

Q6. Write the features of a TV station.

Ans. Features of TV station are as follows:

(1) Production Control Room (PCR): Every TV studio is invariably associated with a Production Control Room, which houses all the electronic equipment and operational controls to conduct the 'show'. It is usually located adjacent to the studios, with an observation glass window between the two. From the PCR, the producer (sometimes called Director) of the programme calls the shots, while other technical personnel are engaged in their assigned tasks like camera control, audio control, lights, vision mixing, insertion of external feeds, and recording the programme on a video tape.

The cameramen in the studio handle their individual TV cameras to compose the shots from different angles, in accordance with the 'commands' of the producer. Inter-communication between the producer in the PCR and the cameramen in the studio happens through the handsets, which the cameramen constantly wear during the shooting.

(2) TV Studio: The studio is the place where action takes place and the same is shot with the help of video cameras (usually more than one simultaneously). The floor area of a TV studio ranges from that of a typical living room (~25 square meter) to as much as 400 square meter or even more. Bigger studios are necessary if drama sequences employing elaborate sets and lighting arrangements are to be provided. For other purposes, e.g. news reading, interviews, educational lectures etc., small studios are preferred, because of economic reasons and also because modern technology permits space-saving by way of 'virtual' sets, portable equipment, etc. Most studios in the educational sector and private TV channels adopt this trend.

(3) Set design: Traditionally, sets in a TV studio are constructed by assembling 8ft. X 4 Ft. plywood cutouts in the require shape. Modular set-design containing sub-assemblies, which can easily be dismantled and re-used for different shapes and sizes, is preferred now a days for reasons of economy and easy storage. 'Virtual sets' are those which are created electronically on the TV screen against the background of performers in the studio, with the help of computer-generated imagery. This concept is gaining currency as it can obviate the tedium and the cost involved in traditional set design and construction. In the case, nothing actually exists in the studio, except a blue screen, as the backdrop for the performers. The set is 'created' on the final image by electronically replacing the blue background by the artwork generated with the help of computers. The computer software also provides for perspective changes of the virtual set, as per changes in camera angles, as if in realistic situation.

(4) Computer Graphics and Animation: This is an indispensable facility for educational programmes in particular. Successive advancements in computer technology have resulted in a variety of user-friendly software for graphics and animation which can run on computers. This kind of 'open architecture' has added advantage of easy upgradeability and networked operation within a studio complex.

(5) Outdoor Coverage Facilities: All TV production houses, particularly those involved in news and current affairs programmes, need these facilities in an adequate measure. At the simplest, they consist of a hand-held or shoulder mounted camcorder (portable audio/video recorder) with a built-in microphone and a single person crew. This may be good enough for a quick coverage of a natural disaster, an accident site, etc. for a pre-planned event or documentary production. Otherwise things like portable lighting equipment, tripod-mounted camcorder, wheels and trolley for jerk-free movement of the camera, different kinds of microphones, etc. are used. The size of the crew too many have to be bigger as a producer, a production assistant, cameraman, sound recordist, an electrician, and a helper are needed.

For live coverage of outdoor events, an OB Van (Outdoor Broadcast Van) is used. The technical system in the Van will be similar to that found in the TV studio and control room to facilitate production in real time by a multi-camera set up. In other words, an OB Van can be described as a multi camera set up on wheels.

(6) Editing/Post Production Suites: The terms postproduction refers collectively to all the processes that follow in making the final TV programme, after the basic material is shot either within the studios or outdoors. These processes may include putting the wanted shots in the desired sequences, adding the opening and closing shots, laying the commentary track, music mixing graphics/animation sequences and other inserts, and producing the final master tape. The amount of editing and postproduction work depends on the format of the programme. As for instance, drama and documentary programmes involve extensive post production work that may run into several days, while current affairs programmes, educational talks, simple demonstrations, etc. require less postproduction work. Live programmes like news, of course, cannot have any postproduction. However, in their case, editing of news clips, visuals, etc. happens beforehand and they are played back as part of the programme during the telecast.

Q7. What are the transmission techniques used for distribution of television signals?

Or

Discuss advantages and disadvantages of the following means of distribution of television signals to home:

(a) Terrestrial transmission

(b) Satellite distribution

Ans. The three most popular means of distribution of TV signals to homes are as follows:

- Broadcasting through terrestrial (ground-based) transmitters
- Satellite and cable distribution
- Direct-to-Home (DTH) Television via satellite

(1) Terrestrial Transmitters: As in the case of a radio transmitter, a TV transmitter 'modulates the incoming TV signals on to a higher frequency carrier, amplifies the power of the modulated waves and sends them to the aerial system for radiation into space in the form of electromagnetic waves. Since a TV signal is in practice two distinct signals one for the picture and the other for the sound - a TV transmitter is in effect a two-in-one transmitter, which deals with the picture as well as sound transmission in an integrated fashion. Again, while radio transmission takes place in medium wave, shortwave, VHF (glossary) and UHF (glossary) bands, for compelling technical reasons international regulations restrict terrestrial TV to VHF and UHF bands only. Please recall that wave propagation in these bands follows a straight path, which, means that TV signals, like FM radio, travel over line-of-sight (glossary) distances. To maximize the coverage area of a TV station, therefore, the transmitting aerials are located on the top of tall mast in about 60 km radius. In metro cities with many skyscrapers, you need much taller towers to satisfy the line-of-sight requirements within the coverage area. So is the case in hilly areas with many ups and downs. Short towers will do if the area is a flat, rural landscape. For example, in Mumbai, the Doordarshan tower is 300 meters tall. Also, wherever possible, TV towers are located on hill tops, to gain maximum visibility (and therefore coverage) for the transmitting aerial. This is the case in Pune where the TV tower is located on the Sinhagarh hill.

Terrestrial transmissions can be received by TV homes by means of simple 'Yagi' aerial which can be erected on a roof or a balcony. A typical Yagi aerial contain 3 aluminum rods of specific lengths (to suit the wave length of transmission). Out of these, the middle one is folded inwards and is known as a folded di-pole. The transmission picked by the folded dipole are carried to the TV set inside the house through a flat cable called feeder line.

The rod in front of the folded dipole is called 'director' and the one behind is called 'reflector'. Together, they help in maximizing the 'gain' of the aerial in the wanted direction.

Till a decade ago, urban areas in our country were replete with these aerials, sprouting from the rooftops of numerous households, as TV reception would have been impossible without them. Terrestrial transmission of Television is now largely overtaken by satellite and cable because of the phenomenal growth in cable networks in the recent past. For non-cable TV households, however, terrestrial TV continued to be the only lifeline. Therefore, Doordarshan maintains a large fleet of terrestrial transmitters across the country to ensure TV coverage to remote rural communities at affordable cost.

(2) Satellite and Cable Distribution: A chief limitation of terrestrial TV, you will agree, is its limited range, further limited by line-fo-sight propagation. This limited range can be improved to some extent by erecting taller towers and increasing the power of transmitters, but obviously there are limits and terrestrial transmissions cannot be expected to go beyond 100 km even in favourable circumstances. The only way of expanding terrestrial TV coverage across longer distances is by setting up 'repeater' stations, i.e. pickup the signals at the fringe of the coverage area of the original transmitter and re-transmit them through a second transmitter, and so on.

Satellite communication as an economical alternatives to terrestrial repeaters. Communication satellites are man made devices placed at an altitude of about 36,000 km up above the equator, so that they revolve around the earth, much like the moon (earth's natural satellite) revolves around the earth. However, because of the particular altitude of their orbit, communications satellites take exactly 24 hours to complete one revolution, the same time that earth takes to rotate around itself. Any satellite at a lower orbit revolves much faster, while those at higher orbits revolve slower. The time period of 24 hours is unique to this particular orbit which is known by the name 'geo-stationary orbit', because the satellites in this orbit appear stationary as seen from the earth. Communications satellites receive the signals sent towards them from the ground and, after necessary frequency conversion and amplification, retransmit them back earthward, so that they can be received by a suitably equipped dish antenna located within the 'foot print' (that is, coverage area) of the satellite. Since a single satellite can 'see' as much as one-third of the earth's surface, a compliment of just three satellites can provide global coverage of television, cutting across national boundaries and continents.

The transmission side of a typical satcom system consists of an 'earth station' to which the programmes generated by the studio center are sent. The earth station contains necessary electronic equipment to 'uplink' (that is, transmit upwards to the satellite) the signals in the desired frequency band, with the help of a large dish antenna which is accurately kept directed to the satellite in the sky. Once adjusted, the dish remains pointed towards the satellite all the time. So it does not need to be disturbed except for very occasional perturbations. Presently, maximum number of satellite TV channels the world over operates in the so called 'C' band (4 to 6 GHz range). However, as this band is already crowded, 'Ku' band (12 to 18 GHz) is the new frequency band which is rapidly gaining currency for upcoming TV channels, as well as for DTH.

The receiving system is known by the acronym DRS (Direct Reception System) which consists of a dish antenna (typical size 8 to 12 ft. diameter) fitted with a feed-horn and LNBC (Low Noise Block Converter) at its focus. When the earthward transmission from the satellite falls on the dish, the electromagnetic waves get reflected to coverage at its focus. A 'feed-horn' mounted at this point collects the energy and feeds the LNBC.

The LNBC performs the dual task of amplification and conversion of high frequencies, to similar signals carried at a much lower frequency. These lower frequencies travel through cables and is then fed to a satellite receiver. It is the job of the satellite receiver to process the received signals into a form which can be handled by the domestic TV set, which is kept connected to the output of the satellite receiver.

Most satellite TV channels as of now adopt digital transmission techniques to economize on the satellite transponder space. Therefore the satellite receiver employed in the DRS should be a digital one. Such receivers are known by the technical term Integrated Receiver Decoder (IRD). Digital satellite TV channels also often employ 'scrambling' techniques, so that only authorized IRD are activated for de-scrambling the signals. For example, most of the private TV channels like DD (Doordarshan) and Gyandarshan are free-to-air, without any scrambling.

(3) DTH (Direct to Home Television): Direct to home (DTH) television service, also known as direct broadcast satellite service, is becoming popular in India. In March 2001, the government allowed Ku-band direct to home television broadcasting by issuing a notification and laying down the ground rules for companies wanting to enter DTH in India. DTH is the technology that allows people to receive television programmes directly via satellite, using a small dish antenna. The user can receive DTH broadcasts without having to depend on cable TV providers. The KU-band DTH service offers greater and direct connectivity to the viewers providing access to 100 channels through a small dish antenna.

DTH has arrived which is a satellite based television broadcasting. The primary difference between the normal satellite based television and DTH is the transmission band allocation for these services. The DTH service operates or Ku-band, which is different from the C-band currently employed by the satellite TV broadcasters. The main advantage of the new DTH system is the size of the antenna required to receive the signal, which is much smaller in size. For Ku band, dish of about 35 to 40 centimeters in diameter can be used. The antenna is small and light enough to mount it on the terrace/balcony/bracket of a window and connect it to TV set with a cable. The DTH signal as such is not suitable for feeding directly to a TV receiver and it must be passed through a small receiver (a set top box) before feeding to the television set.

Since, DTH system can accommodate over 100 channels, the direct-to-home TV service providers will offer a bouquet of channels, much as the cable operator does now. Like existing pay TV channels, DTH transmission can only be received if the subscriber has paid a fee. The authorization may come in the form of the SIM cards currently being used to sell airtime to mobile phone users. Slipping this "smart card" into the set top box will unlock the service for a given number of hours. When the purchased time is exhausted subscribers shall have to buy another card to renew the service.

While promising enhanced picture quality, DTH also has the scope for interactive television and value-added services like

- Movie on demand
- Internet access
- Home shopping
- Banking
- Tele-education

Q8. What are the new trends that are emerging today in broadcasting?

Ans. Technological advancements have been giving more and more advanced technology in every aspect of our lives i.e., education, entertainment, medical, etc. Once we have any technology, we will get its advanced version soon. So emerging trends in broadcasting are as follows:

(1) Digital Terrestrial Television (DTT): While the traditional TV transmission is terrestrial analogue, DTT is digital. To receive DTT, you need a set top box before your TV set. Doordarshan has DTT mode in the four metro cities already. Apart from superior picture and sound quality, the real advantage of DTT lies in the value-added services it can offer to the viewers: video-on-demand, tele-shopping, program-related services, etc.

(2) Campus Radio: At the other end of the scale, the concept of highly localized broadcasting with a coverage area of no more than 5 km radius, is also gaining currency. Educational institutions can set up their own radio station at minimal cost to serve their respective campuses and neighborhood. Campus Radio can be used to promote community life, student welfare activities, supplementary educational lessons beyond classroom hours, counselling through distance mode, career guidance, cultural activities etc.

(3) Webcasting: The universal reach of the internet and World Wide Web has enabled broadcasters to adopt this medium to reach out specific audiences irrespective of geographical boundaries and, in the process, take advantage of the value-added features that only the web casting mode can offer. Unlike conventional broadcasts, webcasting enables viewers/listeners to access their chosen programmes at a time of their convenience on their computer sets and repeatedly if desired. Access can be restricted by the broadcaster as per their marketing strategy: say pay-per-view, as per monthly/yearly subscription etc.

Many leading sound broadcasters around the world (including All India Radio) have their web casting channels. But television channels on the web are still not so prolific because of technical reasons like non-availability of sufficient bandwidth at many places. In the absence of adequate bandwidth, web cast pictures tend to lack definition and be jerky, unclear and go into freeze now and then.

(4) Digital Audio Broadcasting (DAB) through Satellites: Digital Audio Broadcasting (DAB) through satellites enables global coverage and also CD like quality for audio broadcasts. Thus, DAB is an efficient solution for the problems of quality as well as quantity at one stroke. However, the disadvantage is that ordinary radio sets cannot work for DAB; you need special sets which are quite expensive for the common man. The 'Worldspace' radio is an example of satellite based DAB. With a fleet of three satellites, Worldspace aims to provide high fidelity programmes to global audiences. In the context of education, DAB can have interesting applications for distance education institutions that wish to offer their programmes for learners dispersed across continents.

(5) Briefcase radio: A briefcase radio is a radio station that is so simply designed and compact that it can fit into a briefcase. It is being used in some places as a community radio to share the local news, knowledge and problems. The community is active in the production and broadcast of such programmes. The programme shave a limited reach but serve the purposes of the community quite well. It has been successfully used in some places like Gujarat, Karnataka, Andhra Pradesh., etc.

Q9. Discuss the concept of video studio. What the main equipments used in video studio?

Ans. The video studio is used for both the broadcast as well as for the non-broadcast mode. In the broadcast mode the productions are transmitted from the studio. On the other hand video programmes can also be recorded and then edited to make the master program. These master programmes can also be transmitted in the broadcast mode. In the non-broadcast mode the master program after the final preview is mass duplicated into the analog or the digital video format. These recordings are then sent to the students, who can play them back at their home/workplace or can access them at study centers with audio-video library. In this section you will come to know about the video studio used for recording. The video studio is divided into the following two parts:

(1) Studio floor: The video studio floor is the main activity centre for the video program. Depending upon the format of the program sets, microphones, lights and camera etc. are placed in the studio floor.

(2) Control rooms: The control room has various equipments installed such as those for vision mixing, audio mixing, lighting control, video recorders/playback, camera control units, video type writer, caption scanner, computer, video monitors, waveform monitors (used to measure and display the level, of a video signal with respect to time, amplifiers speakers, etc.

The size of the studio depends upon several factors such as the equipments used, the number of the cameras to be used and also depends upon the format of the program it is expected to handle. In major television organizations, video studios of requisite sizes are earmarked for specific programming needs. The video studio sizes in the range of 75 to 200 sq. m floor areas are suitable for educational program production. Studios of still larger sizes would find more utility for the public television and entertainment programming.

A rectangular shape for the studio floor rather than exact square is preferred in order that the floor area may be best utilized for camera movement and set erection. A square shape tends to give rise to unfavourable acoustics. The ceiling height is a critical requirement for the video studios. The minimum height required is governed by the considerations like vertical space needed for air conditioning ducts, proper angles for studio lighting in the vertical plane, etc.

Main Equipments in Video Studio: There are several types of equipments used for a multi camera video production, some of the major ones are discussed below:

(1) Digital Video Effect (DVE): Digital video effect equipment can be used either as a stand alone unit or in conjunction with the production switches, although the latter method is preferred in most production houses. The common terms to describe this class of effects are: compression, expansion, split screen, freeze, perspective, rotation, reversal, posterization, page turn, roll and slide.

The consideration that can be kept in view while choosing digital effects equipment are - the range of effects that it can provide, whether the effects are easy to set up and repeat at will, whether the picture edges and movements are sufficiently smooth, resolution and other specification determining picture quality.

In general it is desirable to locate DVE facilities at the postproduction stage rather than at the studio, as to operate the required effects in live situations would be rather difficult. Also, beware of the fact that any overuse of these effects in educational programming can be visually distracting and counter productive.

(2) Lighting: Lighting plays a very important role in television. It illuminates the camera 'to see' and 'record' a subject or scene clearly and distinctly. It also helps to provide an illusion of depth, giving a three-dimensional effect to otherwise two dimensional images. For complex productions, several lights of varied intensity may be required.

(3) Production switcher (Vision Mixer): It is the control to any video studio set up and most of the post production situation. It is a device used to select among different video sources and in some cases mix them and add special effects. A significant special effect that professional grade production switches provide is the "Chroma key", with the help of which the plain background of a person (usually blue colored background) can be electronically replaced by any other video content-live or pre-recorded.

(4) Video Camera: Video cameras meant for use in studio or outdoor functions contain CCD (Change couple device) chips to convert light into electrical signal. It stores and displays the data for an image in such a way that each pixel in the image is converted into an electrical charge. With suitable changes in accessories, it is possible to use the same video camera in studio and for outdoor shooting. Nowadays the camcorder (Camera plus recorder in a single casing or as a removable attachment) has become the preferred system for outdoor shooting. Its advantage is that a single person crew may carry out the shooting, which may also include audio as narration, music, etc.

(5) Video cassette recorder (VCR): VCR provides facilities for recording and playback of removable video tape cassettes containing magnetic tape used for recording audio and video.

Q10. Describe various presentation formats of the video programme.

Ans. There are various presentation formats of the video programme. Some of them are:

(1) Interview: A wide variety of situations can be termed interviews. Personality chat, format round-the table discussions, explanatory discussions, reminiscences, etc. may be presented through interviews. Famous TV interview programme like the question time, hard talk are the typical examples.

(2) Illustrated talk: In addition to the talk there are visuals illustrating it as for example, a person working in a laboratory, museum, etc.

(3) Talk shows: A single person may talk/lecture. There can be also be those who express their 'dissent' to the speakers with two or more speakers and one who anchors. For instance, debates among people holding conflicting views, panel discussions where each panelists presents his/her views, etc.

(4) Discussion: It covers all talk shows like interviews, panel discussions, etc. and even the audience may participate in such discussions.

(5) Game shows: Competitions that could be academic as quizzes or those involving physical strength and stamina, etc. comprise game shows.

(6) Demonstrations: These can be used to show a process, actions and reactions. For example how to provide first aid to an accident victim, or a show that teaches horticultural skills. Videotaping has the advantage that the 'perfect' version is recorded and shown and ensures a convincing and controlling demonstration. You can even present action in a speeded-up or slowed-down form, or stop it in a "freeze-frame" to study a particular feature.

Q11. Write the production stages of video programmes.

Ans. The different stages involved in the production of videos can be discussed as follows:

(1) Preproduction Stage: The preproduction stage deals with the preparation of the program proposal, academic note, idea, premises, synopses, treatments, script development, script development, script breakdowns, production schedule, and storyboard. The program proposal is generated after research and extensive discussion with the producer and the academic experts. The proposals should contain the title, the target audience, the justification, the program objectives and an outline of the content and the treatment.

Research is undertaken at the initial stages of the program proposal and a synopsis, which briefly describes the basic story line/theme is prepared. The treatments are longer descriptions with summaries accompanied with pictures depicting a premise.

(i) **TV Script:** A script is then written for the video program. It relates words (which may be a simple summary or a detailed script of the commentary and/or the presenter's words) to the storyboard. It should contain carefully researched material and should be complete as far as possible to prevent tedious script in the fact that it contains comments for video and audios as well. This is normally divided into two halves. Left side of the sheet for video related descriptions and the right side for audio.

In the preparation of the script and its associated documents, various individual styles are used. The following are the typical example that are most commonly used in script preparation:

(a) **Synopsis:** This is general outline of the program idea. In a drama, it may accompany the script to give a rapid summary of the plot, action, character, etc.

(b) **Break down shot/show format:** It lists the items or program segments in a show in the order they are to be shot. It may show duration of the participation, shot numbers, etc. The program may start with the opening titles and music for few seconds. It will then show the program introduction followed by the detailed program and in the end it will show the end titles.

(c) **Story board:** The storyboard is presented on specially designed paper with areas representing a TV screen and a place below the screen for Video and Audio cues. The areas appearing like TV screens will contain rough drawings of the camera shot as planned and how the frame would look to the viewer. The storyboard will also contain issues like backgrounds used, characters, lighting descriptions, dialogue, etc.

A storyboard helps put your ideas across, before undertaking the shooting of the program. It helps the whole team visualize the complete production. Another use of the storyboard is that it gives all the personnel involved with the production, a clear understanding of the events that are to take place and the sequence of the shoot. Cameramen understand what angles they have to position their cameras, whether they need to take a close-up shot or a medium shot or a long shot.

(2) Production Stage: At this stage all the planning processes and the pre-production tasks converge and the functioning of full production team comes into play. The producer holds the production meeting before the actual recording of the programme. It is attended by the production assistants, cameraman, lighting supervisor, technical director, sound engineer, vision mixer operator, VTR operator, property designer, etc. The producer discusses the production script and the floor plan prepared by the set designer, circulated to the cameraman. All the technical issues (lighting and the selection and the placement of the microphones etc.) are discussed with the technical director and the other technical operations staff and finalized with the producer.

Before the actual recording the producer should supervise the following aspects:

- Set has been properly erected and placing of all the things, like furniture, decorative pieces, etc. as required for sets are completed.
- The lighting in the Studio are done as per the requirements.
- Cameras have been aligned properly with the help of CCU and are positioned in the studio floor. Camera cards have been fixed on each of the cameras.
- All the necessary Audio/Video tapes used for the playback and recording are being handed over to the VTR engineer.
- Microphone and the other technical equipment checked by the technical director are put in the proper places.
- The credits (name of script writer, editor, producer, etc.) have been entered in the Video type writer (VTW) or computer.
- The production and the technical crew members have taken up their respective tasks and positions.

(i) **Reading and rehearsal:** This stage involves the reading of the script, timing the length of the program, correcting for pronunciation, articulation, language and experimenting with camera angles. Rehearsals are important as they save valuable TV production time by identifying possible errors and correcting them. The producer will concurrently assesses his production, guides cameras into the shots he is seeking, and works out substitute treatment where necessary. A proper reading and rehearsal is rewarding as it minimizes studio costs.

(ii) **Video recording:** Once the program has been thoroughly read and rehearsed it can be recorded. This involves the producer, production assistant, cameraman, floor manager, vision mixing engineer, sound engineer, microphones, video recorders, etc. Recording is carried out under the direction of the producer who is ably assisted by the production assistant and the floor manager. The video production is shot as a sequence of takes with a crew member logging good and no good takes using time code as a reference. This will be used in the editing process.

(3) Post-production: Postproduction beings after the audio and the videos have been recorded in the tape. It now requires proper editing to make the master program.

(i) **Editing:** Once the recording process is over the video and audio recording material is moved into an editing room. Editing rooms can comprise of linear type editing suites or the more modern Non linear editing workstations depending on the availability and costs. Here mistakes, improper takes, unwanted visuals and sounds that were recorded in the recording process are cleaned up. Additional elements like graphic elements that could not be added at the time of the shoot are inserted here. Video could be acquired from a multi location shoot and these are then pieced together using the storyboard as a reference. Sound effects and music as needed by the program are added and mixed to form the composite audio track.

(ii) **Preview:** At the end of editing the final program a preview is held to evaluate the program and carry out changes if found necessary. If there are changes necessary the program will go back for editing. The master tape now ready is used for broadcast, duplication or is stored in a suitable library.

Q12. Write short notes on the following:

(i) Storage

Ans. Proper storage of audio video materials produced is important. Proper environmental conditions should be ensured in the place where they are stored. Humidity, high temperature, dust, textile particles, harsh chemicals, strong magnetic fields, direct sunlight, lights of certain frequencies, can be harmful. It is better to put the tapes and CDs, DVDs, etc. in their cases to prevent mechanical damages, especially scratches. Dropping them or shaking them can also damage them. Tapes are especially delicate and should not be meddled with. Rewinding them should be done carefully. Misalignments and careless fitting while playing them could damage them severely. Finger prints from touching them leads to sticky patches that attract dust. It is important to ensure that the storage space is fireproof, thermally insulated and is not vulnerable to water and dampness. The storage area should be air conditioned. Nowadays the racks and vaults used for storage are metallic and not wooden. The cassettes and discs should be stored upright. The master copies should not be easily accessible to once and all but should be in the custody of trained people. The replay equipments should be properly maintained. However, in spite of all precautions, data carriers could be damaged. Even digitally stored data may be lost. Replay instruments could also damage the data carrier. Even normal replaying on repeated occasions may damage them. Hence, it is always better to maintain backup copies. It is also important that replay machine and the recorded formats are compatible with each other. With obsolesce of replay machines, the new machines may not be able to read the data stored in the older formats which then becomes useless. Let us discuss a simple example. New models of computers may not be able to read the data we had stored in floppies. Hence it is necessary to keep pace with obsolescence and transfer data in a format that the new machines will replay.

(ii) Archiving

Ans. Archiving audio/video means they would be stored for a long time. We see some old films that have now poor audio and video quality. But good films, audios, videos have to be stored properly for future generations. The data may be stored in analog or digital form. Unless storage is done properly the archived materials may lose quality. Nowadays computers help in the processes related to the preservation of data i.e. archiving. To ensure the retention of quality and allow subsequent replay, the data (audio/video) is digitized, compressed and then stored in an intermediate archive format (IAF). Indexing and cataloguing are also required for subsequent searching of the audio/video content. This is because as the archive grows in size, searching the data becomes difficult. Indexing helps us to create path to the data stored. Conventionally, creating a few key words for annotating the data is done. But today more advanced techniques that make retrieval of the data stored easier are available. Cataloguing as is done in libraries for printed materials, is the process of systematically listing the items available. It includes preparing a formal description of the audio-video tapes and titles. This could include a title, a brief description of the content, the location of recording, etc. These information help in easily locating a particular audio/video form those stored.

Q13. What are the limitations and advantages of non-broadcast media in audio and video?

Ans. Limitations of the non-broadcast media: The following are the main limitations of non-broadcast media.

(1) Audio/video cassettes require costly recording and presentation equipment.

(2) Due to the availability of the variety of format (Analog/Digital) and systems, which are essentially incompatible, the choice of any particular format to record the audio/video programme is very difficult, thereby increasing the complexity of the inventory that has to be maintained for any program.

(3) For an educational programme, they are better as part of an integrated package with print, and other modes of delivering rather than being sufficient in themselves.

(4) With the increasing use of phone-in methodology used in today's broadcast, interaction with the student is easy. The student can clarify the doubts on the spot. With live interactions the program becomes more interesting. Whereas in the non-broadcast mode response is via letters or phone calls or emails asking for clarifications.

Strengths of Non-broadcast Media

(1) Video is effective for course materials which need demonstration/visual illustrations which cannot be taught effectively through radio and audio cassettes.

(2) To hold attention and motivate the students, the content can be presented in interesting formats, which can help the student retain and recall information presented through the programs.

(3) Educational broadcast is not accorded priority in the radio/television set up. The technical staffs concerned with the planning and production of radio programmes often lack adequate knowledge of the relevant pedagogical needs of the learners and their characteristics. The subject expert at times may not have any deep acquaintance with the complexities of programme production. Hence good quality videos can be assets for learners.

(4) Non-broadcast media can overcome many of the limitations of radio and television broadcast. It provides considerable freedom to the

learners who can use it any time and place at their convenience. Also the pace of delivery can be controlled. The viewer can review the program many times and take their own time to understand the subject.

(5) Programs of a sensitive nature can be used effectively with targeted students through the non-broadcast mode by virtue of the fact that the non-broadcast mode gives them the necessary privacy by limiting the target group to a few individuals or even a single person.

(6) The cassette player is comparatively inexpensive, simple to operate, flexible and portable.

(7) It is a flexible medium. Sufficient time can be allocated to a topic that can be taken up in details.

Q14. Explain the role of teleconferencing in distance learning.

Or

What are the types of teleconferencing/audio conferencing can be used in distance learning?

Or

What are merits and demerits of audio technologies?

Ans. Teleconferencing can be defined as meeting through a telecommunications medium. It is a generic term for linking people between two or more locations by electronics. Teleconferencing, using various technologies and combinations of technologies, has been an important mediated form of distance learning. Students who study at a distance are separated both from their tutor and their peers. Social interactions, sharing of ideas, joy of learning and discovering together, sharing successes and failures and general social support are all to a certain extent, missing form distance learning environment.

Teleconferencing is a medium which can counteract this problem of distance learners. The task of distance educator is therefore to obviate these problems as much as possible by using appropriate technologies, maintain a stimulating environment and create opportunities for students to communicate with teachers and with each other on a regular basis.

In teleconferencing a two way communication using electronic equipment between students who are located at separate locations and teacher in a studio can be called "teleconference". Such communication is facilitated by a combination of electronic equipment and communication channels. The communication channels can be simple telephone networks to satellite links. Interaction between teacher and student is achieved by different type of technologies. These technologies are divided as synchronous and asynchronous depending on the nature of communication either live or recorded. Synchronous communication are real time conversations between all participants in the conference. For instance, a radio broadcast received simultaneously by all the listeners, teleconference telecast from IGNOU headquarters to students at study centers via satellite, etc. are examples of this type of communication.

Conferencing helps in the following manners:

(1) make learning interactive, participatory and dialogue based.

(2) facilitates collaborative learning through exchange of information, sharing of resources, team work.

(3) provides a virtual learning environment when access to real experiences is not feasible.

(4) provides equitable access to resources to learners especially to those in rural and remote places.

(5) facilitates rapid access to information.

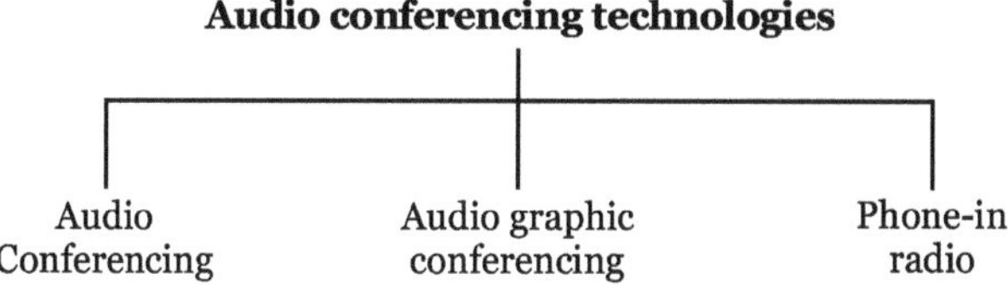

There are following types of audio conferencing:

(1) Audio Graphic Conferencing: Audio conferencing can be improved by value addition by way of sending picture/data along with voice communication. The picture/data information can be sent in advance for use at the time of audio conferencing or it can be sent over a telephone line itself. This mode of conferencing is called audio graphic conferencing. Graphic scanner, electronic white board/electronic tablets with appropriate software can be used to transmit graphics, sketches, etc. Audio Graphic conferencing is also some times referred to as enhance audio or audio plus.

Audio Graphic conferencing is advantageous than mere audio conference as it also transmits visual information. Even though simple static graphic are received by the students, they are of great help in understanding the topic under discussion. These visuals bring clarity in explanation of the subject. Sometimes we may be required to use separate lines to transmit the voice and visuals for better interactions.

(2) Phone in Radio: Phone-in radio is very popular nowadays. Every one in the vicinity of FM broadcast might have heard one or the other phone-in programs. In phone in radio, the communication is point to multipoint by radio broadcast to the learners and the interaction is through a simple telephone line. Teachers at the studio of the broadcasting station teach and answer the queries raised by learners, who dial into the studio telephone numbers using ordinary telephone. To encourage students to interact freely, these numbers can be toll free i.e. students need not pay for the calls made. Voice of the students on telephone is also mixed and broadcast therefore everybody listening to the programme is also benefited by the discussion. Phone in radio virtually creates a classroom spread over large area covered by the radio broadcast. For example IGNOU conducts interactive radio counseling program with the help of All India Radio national network, which can be heard through out the country. Government of India is encouraging universities to install FM radio stations for campus broadcasts. These low power stations can boost Phone-in radio use in education sector. Equipment needed by the student to participate in Radio Phone in program is only radio receiver and Telephone. Fax machines also be used to communicate during such programmes to send text and sketches if required.

Merits and Demerits of Audio Technologies: The merits and demerits of audio conferencing are as follows:

Merits

- Equipment required to setup audio conference is simple and less expensive.
- Options for selecting Telephone or speaker phones and a telephone networks are many.
- Audio conference can be easily recorded by the students themselves for reference.
- Students can participate in the conference from anywhere.

Demerits

- Difficult to explain abstract concepts one audio conference due to lack of visual information.

- It is difficult to learn through audio information only.
- Scheduling is necessary and needs coordination between teacher availability and student convenience.
- Since eye contact is not possible it is difficult to retain attention of students.

(3) Audio conferencing: Simple conversation on telephone by more than two persons may be treated as 'Audio Conferencing'. Nowadays many telephone networks and modern hand sets can offer this facility. While conversation between two people is a point to point communication, by using conferencing facility a telephone network can be used for multipoint communication. Such conference facilities can be used in distance teaching easily as they are simple to set up. They can be setup by dialing the number designated for conference by each students. However as the number of students connected to the system increases the quality of the sound may reduce. To overcome this situation a special equipment known as 'Audio Bridge' is developed.

Audio Bridge is designed to connect number of telephones so that people from different places can converse simultaneously. This bridge electronically mixes the audio signals from the connected telephone line from various locations. The circuitry in the bridge balance the signals level and also isolate/reduce the telephone line noise to provide quality audio. The conference can be set up using bridge either by students dialing the number designated for conference or an operator at conference nodal location connecting to the students required to participate in the audio conference.

In case of student calling into the conference bridge, a telephone number (allotted to special bridge) can be published or sent along with the time schedule of the conference. The telephone number can be toll free number (see glossary) to encourage participation. In this type of conference each student has to dial in as per the schedule. In case of an operator connecting, each and every participating student located at different location will be dialed from the bridge equipment. The limitation in such a system could be that a list of the numbers of the students is required and a student has to be present at the same location during conferencing. While standard telephone set can be used for participating audio conference, better designed speaker phone can be used for hand free conversation. It is also good idea to install amplifier in the hall where more students are assembled, at a given center. The center can have acoustically treated hall for better audio quality.

Q15. Define the types of video conferencing which can be used in distance learning.

Or

Write the merits and demerits of video conferencing.

Ans. Video conferencing, also can be called video teleconferencing is setup using both audio and video equipments for transmission as well as reception from separate locations. This set up allows student to see the teacher and his/her presentation and interact with him/her. Unlike audio graphic conferencing, in video conferencing video cameras are used for transmitting moving pictures. Video conferencing is set up either between point to point through a telephone network and equipments for compressing and decompressing the audio video signals or it can be point to multi point by using broadcasting equipments.

Video conferencing systems can be divided broadly into two types

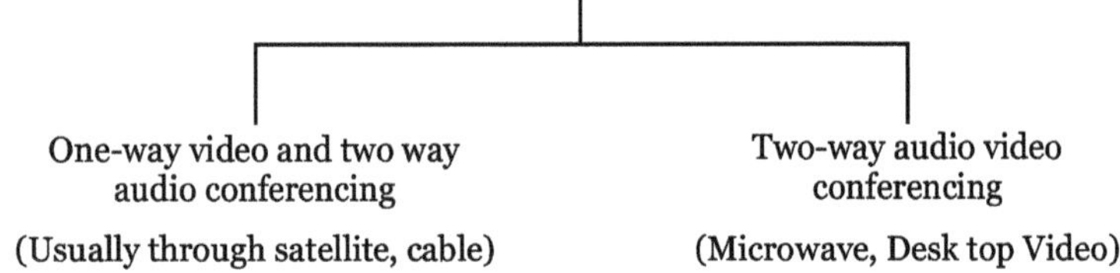

(1) Two-way audio video conferencing: In this type of conference audio and video signals are exchanged between teaching studio and receiving center. The two way conference can be point to point or between multiple locations. The receiving center can receive pictures and audio from other centers. All centers are equipped to send and receive video and audio viz. cameras, microphones and monitors.

There are following types of two-way audio video conferencing:

(i) **Microwave Television Conferencing:** While, Satellites are popular for enabling video communications over long distances, microwave transmissions provide a cost-effective method for videoconferencing within more localized areas. Microwave systems are designed to transmit good quality video signals to areas that are not more than 40 km apart. They provide in line of sight (without physical obstacles to block the signals) point-to-point communications. Microwave stations operate at a lower power, require comparatively relatively less expensive equipment. One problem of microwave communication is the availability of limited number of channels in the spectrum in any one area. Microwave communications are not popular for providing education in India.

(ii) **Digital (Desktop) Videoconferencing:** This technology involves the capturing, manipulation and storage of video in digital formats. Desktop videoconferencing uses a computer along with a camera and microphone at one site to transmit video and audio to a computer at another site or sites. The computers involved in digital videoconferencing, require a videoconferencing board (codec board) with the ability to compress and decompress the digitized video. This technique is less expensive than satellite or microwave systems. The disadvantages are that visuals of rapid movements may be of lower quality and that fast transmission lines as Integrated Services Digital Network (ISDN) are required. Slower transmission lines can affect quality of transmission. They are also not very suitable for large groups with many participants.

(2) One-way video and two way audio conferencing: In this type of conference. Students (participants) at multiple sites can see the teacher, but the teacher can not see them except those physically present in the location (studio). Satellite transmission is used in India for one way video and two way audio type of teleconferences. Such teleconferences are used when instructions are to be provided at multiple locations across a wide geographical area. Distance learning through this kind of conference needs a teaching end studio equipped with video cameras, microphones and other mixing equipment. Final studio signals are transmitted to satellite for broadcast or to a cable network system.

The receiving sites/learning centers will have down linking equipment to receive the satellite signals through a small dish or directly from cable and displayed in class rooms/study centers by standard TV sets. Audio interaction with teacher is provided by the use of an audio bridge at the teaching end and telephone lines at remote classrooms.

This point is the part of 2 point so type it as a support of 2nd point and give:

(i) **Satellite based conferencing:** Satellite transmission is best suited for point to multi point communication. Normally a large sized dish with satellite transmitting equipment (up-link facility) is installed for sending audio video signals to satellite at the teaching center. At the receiving centers relatively simple receiving equipment with small size dish is installed.

Many educational institutions may not be in a position to set up up-link and down link equipment on their own. However, these institutions may use facilities set up by the government at certain locations. One example of an educational system that makes use of satellite communication in India is training and development communication channel (TDCC) coordinated by ISRO and IGNOU. Such conferences are being organized on Gyan Darshan, the educational television channel of India. The return audio channel is usually through telephone network and it is also possible via satellite with additional equipment.

You may have noticed similarity with the phone-in radio service and satellite-based conference as both of them use broadcast media to send the educational program. Even though the broadcast is at a scheduled time, students can tape the programme and play it back at a convenient time.

(ii) **Cable Network Based Conference:** Cable networks are set up to bring entertainment satellite channels to homes. This type of cable connection can be used to transmit one-way video and one-way audio transmission to the community at large or between specific locations/receive centers. Cable network based conference will be effective in local area or small townships. In one school/collage, the teacher would teach while in the others, the students can access the television program.

Cable companies will soon be able to use the technology of digital video to offer hundreds of channels to each home and school. Although many of these channels will be used for commercial entertainment purpose, it is expected that a couple of channels will become available for education.

Two-way audio video conferencing (Microwave, desktop conferencing facilities)

For two-way audio video conferencing both teaching and learning ends should have similar equipment to send and receive audio as well as video. Usually microwave TV conferencing are point-to-point communications whereas desk top conferencing can be used for multi point communications.

Advantage/Disadvantages of Video Technologies: Advantage/disadvantages of the video conferencing are summarized as follows:

Advantages

(i) Encourage interactive learning.

(ii) Allow both audio and video communications. Hence it is suitable for teaching that involves demonstrations. Video medium supports visuals related to lab experiments and animations and thus explain abstract topics.

Disadvantages

(i) Requires teachers trained to teach through this technology, and requires a crew with camera men and other technical experts. Effective programmes require rehearsals with teachers and technical team.

(ii) The programmes are scheduled and learners need to be present at the time of transmission.

(iii) It is expensive and the infrastructure at each site may be unaffordable for many institutions.

Q16. Discuss the types of computer conferencing technologies.

Or

Write the merits and demerits of computer conferencing technologies.

Ans. Computer conferencing can be referred to a special kind of electronic communication system which employed to facilitate group discussion over a computer network. As a communications medium useful for group discussion, computer conferencing is the instructional technology through which the liberal arts can apply computers while retaining their identity. This new medium does not replace the teacher but provides an alternative way for teachers and students to meet. Because all communication takes place in natural language, personalities come through clearly and students and teachers really feel that they are in each others' presence. Because all the students in the class see each others' comments and ideas, a feeling of group membership develops, and students frequently are able to learn as much from each other as from the teacher. In its application to video and correspondence courses, computer conferencing adds group interaction to the other advantages of distance learning, with its potential for self-pacing and continuing education.

In computer conferencing, computers are connected by local area network (LAN) or internet. Access to computer conferencing is not limited by time and space, thus offering greater access to student in learning from distance. Computer conferencing allows learners to access information from the teacher and at the same time enables them to interact among themselves. Unlike the audio and videoconferences, computer conferences are mostly text based such as chat rooms and shared white boards. Two types of computer conferencing have been discussed below:

(1) Internet Chat: Internet Chat is a two-way, interactive exchange over the Internet in text mode. In chat mode, two or more people at remote computers connect to the same chat "room" and type messages. Typed messages can be seen by all participants on a shared screen. Online chat allows students and teachers to communicate in "real-time." In internet chat, student feels free to communicate in the absence of cameras/microphones but he/she may have to concentrate hard to express in text mode. Shared white boards can be used to communicate through text and graphics with appropriate software tools. Advanced software even allows users at remote sites to share applications.

(2) Internet Chat: Internet video conferencing usually results in a small image and quality of video depends on the band width availability i.e. speed of the internet connection. In most cases, a regular modern is far too slow to transmit effective video. With improvements in technology, it is possible to get better pictures and sound across internet that can be viewed full screen with better lip-sync i.e. synchronization between lips and sound.

Advantages/Disadvantages of Computer Technologies: Advantages and disadvantages of computer technologies are as follows:

Advantages:

- In computer conferencing usage of text make student more attentive and make them feel free without camera fear.
- The Internet gives world wide access with minimum cost. Teaching is possible internationally in true sense.
- Computers allow students to learn at their own pace and review as often as they like.
- With the use of multimedia, learning can be made interesting and interactive

Disadvantages

- In spite of great developments in computer technology there could be some uncertainty in connectivity or availability of the servers in some places.
- Even though the speed of network connectivity is improving day by day, it is still not fully sufficient to meet video conferencing demands. Therefore communication is still mainly by text.
- Availability of regular power supply is one of the main problems in some areas besides access to computer hardware and desired software.
- Tackling computer viruses is not easy.

Q17. Write the procedure of conducting teleconferencing sessions.

Ans. Teleconferencing can be through the following procedures:

(1) Preparation before conference:

- Create an agenda, call outline or program and make sure all participants have a copy before the teleconference.
- Work in a question and answer session or other participant contribution segment.
- If appropriate, consider sending out a call for questions and feedback prior to the teleconference so participant input can be worked into the agenda.
- Send out support materials prior to the call so participants can print or review them ahead of time.
- Schedule a start and end time for the call and stick to the schedule.

- Consider time zones before scheduling the call to make sure it's convenient for all participants.
- Provide all of the necessary dial-in information, including various time zone translations, at least one day before the call.
- Consider recording the call for people unable to attend or to help in creating a meeting recap after the call.
- Send out a meeting reminder 2-3 days prior to the call.

(2) Preparing Your Equipment:

- Plan to use a landline telephone, if possible, to ensure good quality (and encourage participants to do the same).
- Get a good headset if you plan to use a VoIP connection and test it prior to the call.
- Limit as much background noise as possible.
- Know how to mute your connection and tell participants how to do the same.
- Avoid speaker phone to avoid echoes and clarity challenges.
- Test your connection and call features (such as recording) prior to the live call.
- Have a backup method to connect to the call, just in case.

(3) Conducting the Teleconference:

- Appoint a moderator to make introductions, keep on-task and facilitate the call.
- Appoint someone to take notes during the call.
- Set ground rules for the call if there will be more than three participants to avoid talking over each other.
- Start on time, and delay no longer than five minutes if participants are late to dial in.

(4) After the Teleconference:

- Provide a recap and overview of next steps with specific responsibilities at the end of the call.
- Touch base with participants after the call to get their feedback on how it went and what can be improved for next time.
- Send a written recap and/or meeting minutes to participants after the call.

Q18. What is sound wave? Discuss how does it generate or occur.

Ans. Sound waves are the vibrations that pass through air or any object or material. These waves are actually produced when the sound hits with the materials and objects and vibration is created as a result of this collision. The experts suggest that sound is produced when the frequency of sound is increased or decreased up to certain levels. For example the ears of humans can hear a specific sound frequency. There are different frequencies of sound waves that affect the capabilities of the organisms to hear them.

A vibrating object generates sound by agitating air around it. The vibrating object could be any thing such as - the vocal chord of a person, the membrane of a "tabla" or the vibrating diaphragm of a loudspeaker. The sound generated so, propagates in the form of waves through air. We may describe wave as a disturbance in the air that travels from one location to another location. These sound waves on reaching our ears cause sensation of hearing. Similarly, a microphone, picks up these sounds and converts them into electrical signals analogous (similar) to the sound waves falling on it. A typical sound wave is depicted in Figure.

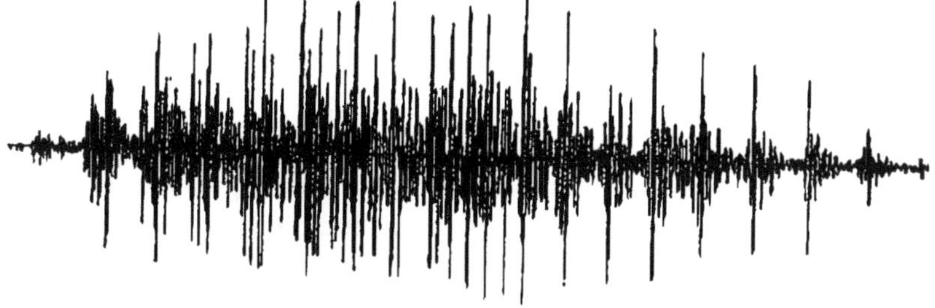

Fig. 4.1: A typical sound wave

The vibrations of the sound generating object are carried by the sound waves. These vibrations in a sound wave when measured as number of cycles (vibrations) per second are known as frequency of the sound. The unit of measurement of frequency is hertz (hz) where one hertz means one cycle per second. Similarly 300hz means 300 cycles per second. As we measure weights in grams, kilograms and Quintals, frequencies are expressed in hertz, kilohertz (khz.) and Megahertz (mhz.) where 'k' means one thousand and 'm' signifies one lakh (100000).

Q19. Write the types of audio signals.

Or

Differentiate between analog audio and digital audio. Mention the advantages of digital audio.

Ans. The types of audio signal can be discussed as follows:

(1) Analog audio signal: An analog audio signal is an electrical waveform which is a representation of the velocity of a microphone diaphragm. Such a signal is two-dimensional in that it carries a voltage changing with respect to time. In analog systems, these waveforms are conveyed by some infinite variation of a continuous parameter. In a recorder, distance along the medium is a further, continuous, analog of time. It does not matter at what point a recording is examined along its length, a value will be found for the recorded signal. That value can itself change with infinite resolution within the physical limits of the system.

In the analog recording process, a duplicate, or electromagnetic representation, of the sound wave of the original sound source can be stored on magnetic tape. For example, a microphone coverts sound pressure changes to changes in voltage that are sent down the microphone cable and recorded onto audio tape as changes in magnetic strength. Each time the analog signal to degradations because the signal changes shape slightly. Analog encoding is similar to creating a line graph to show a statistical analysis. All measurements are on a continuous line that curves up and down with no discrete points. The recording process is like trying to retrace a curve on a graph; the reproduction is always slightly different than the original. In addition to this generation loss, because, analog recording relies on magnetic pulses stored on tape, any defect or decrease in the magnetic properties of the tape means a loss of signal quality. Typical problems for analog recording have included noise and distortion, print-through and crosstalk, flutter and hiss, and limited dynamic range.

The means of representation may be electrical, mechanical, magnetic, electromagnetic, or optical. The amplitude dimension of the audio signal is represented by means of a direct analogy between a voltage, displacement of position (such as for the phonograph or an analog optical sound track), or strength of magnetic flux (analog tape recording), for example, and the signal. Analog systems may also employ modulation and demodulation such as frequency modulation (FM), in which audio is imposed on a carrier frequency, such as a radio frequency, by means of modulation; despite the modulation/demodulation cycle, the audio remains in analog form because no digitization has occurred.

Analog audio is distinguished from digital audio by the fact that analog systems do not use quantization. This means that the representation is intended to be continuous in the amplitude domain. On the other hand, analog audio may be sampled, which is generally considered to be a digital audio process, but if the audio remains unquantized it is not digital audio. An example of a device that uses sampling but not quantizing is the bucket brigade analog delay line, often used in the past for inexpensive audio delay.

(2) Digital audio: Digital audio is simply an alternative means of carrying an audio waveform. Although there are a number of ways in which this can be done, there is one system, known as pulse code modulation (PCM), which is in virtually universal use. Instead of being continuous, the time axis is represented in a discrete, or stepwise manner. The audio waveform is not carried by continuous representation, but by measurement at regular intervals. This process is called sampling and the frequency with which samples are taken is called the sampling rate or sampling frequency F_s. Each sample still varies infinitely as the original waveform did. To complete the conversion to PCM, each sample is then represented to finite accuracy by a discrete number in a process known as quantizing.

At the ADC (analog-to-digital convertor), every effort is made to rid the sampling clock of jitter, or time instability, so every sample is taken at an exactly even time step. Clearly, if there is any subsequent timebase error, the instants at which samples arrive will be changed and the effect can be detected. If samples arrive at some destination with an irregular timebase, the effect can be eliminated by temporarily storing the samples in a memory and reading them out using a stable, locally generated clock. This process is called timebase correction and all properly engineered digital audio systems will use it.

Once sampling is performed, each sample is converted into binary form i.e. a number comprising digits, 0 and 1 only. A single digit, either 0 or 1, is called a bit and a set of eight bits is called a byte. One bit is a datum and many bits are data. How many bits are being used to represent each sample is called resolution of the audio. With lower resolutions there will not be adequate information in the digital signal to represent the original analog sound faithfully and the quality will be poorer. Similar to sampling frequency, higher the resolution higher shall be the audio quality of a recording.

The thumb rules: Audio quality = sampling rate
Audio quality = resolution

Improved audio quality is the major advantage of digital audio but it also has several other advantages over analogue technology. For example, audio effects such as echo, reverberation, etc. can now be performed on a digital audio workstation without requiring complex and expensive analog audio equipment. The quality of audio depends upon several factors. The advantages of digital audio can be discussed as follows:

- **Commercial advantage:** The cost of digital equipment have become quite comparable to its analogue counterparts. Much of digital equipment costs even less and is continuously on the decline. Due to increasing convergence between digital audio and the information technology, the digital audio devices are becoming more economic.

  Though digital audio gives an overall better quality than analog audio, but it suffers from the problem of dropout. It is the momentary loss of audio signal due to the loss of magnetic coating on the tape. Dropouts occur due to wear and tear of the tape as it rubs against the record/playback/erase heads and other tape guiding mechanical systems in a tape recorder. In analog audio recordings dropouts go unnoticed since our ears tend to fill in the gaps, but in digital audio it may lead to absence of a digit thereby changing the meaning of the recorded information which results in producing an altogether different sound i.e. distortion. However, digital error correction methods have been developed reducing this problem to nearly negligible.

- **Sustainable quality:** During tape storage over long periods, the audio signal recorded on magnetic tape gets weakened. The loss of signal strength results in degradation of audio quality. In case of analog audio, the audio quality suffers a lot due to this phenomenon but digital audio is quite less susceptible to it.

In addition to improved sound quality of digital audio due to the factors discussed so far, there are several other benefits associated with digital audio which have contributed to its great success. Some of these factors are:

- **Reduced storage space requirements:** Digital audio recording devices like audio CD, DAT, (Digital Audio Tape), MOD (Magneto Optical Disk) etc. require much less space than the analogue magnetic tape for the same duration of an audio. The DAT cassette is even smaller than domestic audiocassette. Similarly, CD and MOD are much smaller in size but have greater capacity to carry digital audio than old days vinyl records used for storing analog audio.
- **Storage and processing:** Storage and manipulation of digital audio is much easier as compared to its analogue counterpart. This has led to availability of many new recording device and post-production equipment with varied features. Audio work station is one of such systems which makes use of computer based devices for storage and processing of audio in digital format. The analog audio is input to the workstation, which digitizes and then stores digital audio on a hard disk. Editing and efforts can be performed on the stored digital audio on the work station itself with out requiring any additional equipment.

(3) Low noise level: You know that any unwanted sound is known as noise. The magnetic tape used for audio recording has an inherent noise known as tape hiss, which definitely introduces some noise in audio recordings. Though very low noise tapes have been developed but tape noise could not be eliminated completely. Once noise creeps into an audio recording, it can't be removed easily and completely. As compared to analog audio, the digital audio is less susceptible to tape noise because of its different composition (a sequence of 0 and 1).

(4) Generation loss: When one perform an audio recording using a microphone, the recorded material is known as 'first generation' recording. When a 'copy' of the original recording is made by tape to tape transfer, the copy is known as second generation recording. If once again, a new copy is made from the 'second generation' tape, it is known as third generation recording and so on. During each copying process some noise and distortion gets added in the copied version thereby degrading the record audio quality. This degradation of audio quality due to copying process is known as generation loss. As a result, the audio quality suffers on account of reduced frequency response and higher noise. While in analog audio this phenomenon is quite significant but negligible generation loss occurs during copying of digital audio recordings.

Q20. What is Digital Audio Broadcasting (DAB)? Discuss.

Ans. Digital Audio Broadcasting (DAB) was conceived as a means of digitizing audio programmes in order to offer distortion-free reception and CD quality sound. However, the ability of this technology to carry any form of data has allowed it to evolve to convey text, pictures and even video.

Digital radio is like conventional analog radio but is much better in many aspects as given below.

(1) No interference and no re-tuning is required while on move. The digital radio eliminates the noise which plagues the analog audio. Analog radio signals are subject to different kinds of interference on their way from the transmitter to radio receiver. Mountains, high-rise buildings and weather conditions cause these problems. Digital radio reception is virtually immune to interferences because it employs a smart receiver inside which there is a tiny computer. The receiver is capable of re-constructing a solid usable signal out of distorted transmissions. In contrast, an analog receiver cannot differentiate the useful information from the noise.

(2) It offers an improved sound quality. At the listening end, digital radio receivers get sound quality that is significantly better than conventional analog radios, just as audio CD sounds better than earlier Vinyl records (LPs). The crystal clear sound of digital radio is comparable in quality to audio CD.

(3) Transmission of text, data and pictures along with audio. These services are still to be fully utilized but some broadcasters are already broadcasting multi-media radio.

(4) No frequencies are to be remembered which makes tuning of radio easy. With analog radio, you need to tune your radio receiver to the frequency of a radio station e.g. .... MHz for "Gyan Vani" Delhi but the

digital radio receiver displays the names of the stations for you to make a selection.

For the listener, digital radio is an intelligent communications device that offer more services and conveniences than that by conventional analog technology.

Q21. Write short notes on following:

(i) Digital Video

Ans. Digital video can be defined to the capturing, manipulation, and storage of moving images that can be displaced on computer screens. This requires that the moving images be digitally handled by the computer. The word digital refers to a system based on discontinuous events, as opposed to analog, a continuous event. Computers are digital systems; they do not process images the way the human eye does.

Before the Digital Era, to display analog video images on a computer monitor, the video signal had to first be converted from analog to digital form. A special video digitalizing overlay board or hardware on the motherboard had to be installed in your computer to take the video signal and convert it to digital information. To do this, however, required a very powerful computer to be able to read and digitalize every frame repetitively. So the next step in digital video evolution was to eliminate the analog videotape. Thus, the entire procedure, including the capturing of video, is in digital form. First, a camera and a microphone capture the picture and sounds of a video session and send analog signals to a video-capture adapter board. The board only captures half of the number of frames per second that movies use in order to reduce the amount of data to be processed. Second, there is an analog-to-digital converter chip on the video-capture adapter card, and it converts the analog signals (waves) to digital patterns (0s and 1s). Third, a compression/decompression chip or software reduces the data to a minimum necessary for recreating the video signals. In this procedure, no analog was involved, making the process more efficient.

(ii) Digital Television (DTV)

Ans. DTV is more advanced than the older analog technology. Digital Television (DTV) is an advanced broadcasting technology that has transformed the television viewing experience. DTV enables broadcasters to offer television with better picture and sound quality, and multiple channels of programming.

The primary advantage of digital broadcasting is that these binary bits recombine to reproduce an exact copy of the original material. The picture and sound received from a digital transmission are always identical to the original source. Another important benefit of the switch to all-digital broadcasting is that parts of the valuable broadcast spectrum have been freed up for public safety communications by groups such as police, fire departments and rescue squads. Also, some of the spectrum has been auctioned to companies that will be able to provide consumers with advanced wireless services, such as wireless broadband.

Even better, over-the-air digital signals don't weaken over distance, as analog signals do. As long as the signal can be received, the picture is perfect, with no degradation or ghosting. Because digital signals are composed of binary bits, a 1 is always a 1, and a 0 is always a 0. There is no fuzziness or snow in the picture, no ghosts caused by interference.

In addition, digital is a more efficient technology. A digital transmission requires less bandwidth than does a similar analog broadcast; this lets local television stations broadcast two, three, or even four digital channels in the space of a single analog channel. This "multicasting" technology means you'll receive more variety in programming from your local stations—all delivered with superior digital quality.

Q22. Discuss upcoming audio-video delivery technologies.

Ans. As technology is progressively improving from its older versions, it has been giving rich experiences about that since its advent.

In this section we shall discuss some of the upcoming audio video technologies:

- **NICAM stereo-Digital sound for terrestrial television:** NICAM is an abbreviation for Near Instantaneous Companded Audio Multiplex, a system developed for delivering high quality stereo sound on television transmissions. The NICAM stereo, as popularly known, is not only used to deliver a better audio, but it can also be used for sending the data as well. This data could be a picture, text file or any other digitised material.

  The television broadcast carries NICAM stereo sound in addition to analog mono sound to maintain the compatibility with the existing television receivers without NICAM feature.

The audio and data can be sent in several combinations, this allows the user to choose a language out of the two languages being broadcast. Another possibility is to download data while continuing to receive audio as well. The data channel can provide a value added service such as providing supplementary information in the form of text for the video being shown.

- **Satellite Radio:** While on travel suppose you are listening to your favorite radio stations, but when you travel too far away from the source station, you observe the signal breaks and fades. On long trips, when you pass through different cities, you might have to change radio stations every hour or so. However, a satellite radio station broadcasts its signal from more than 35,000 km away in the sky and reaches your car radio with complete clarity allowing you to travel through different cities without having to change the radio station. Satellite radio, offers uninterrupted, near CD-quality music beamed to your radio from space. The major advantages offered by a typical satellite radio station over conventional radio station include the following:

  As discussed earlier, the digital signal means no fading, noise or interference. The system can deliver near CD quality sound, which remains consistent within the coverage area of the satellite.

  The satellite coverage area could be more than 12 million square kilometers without any loss of sound quality

  Generally, digital receiver has a data port that can be connected to personal computer. This enables access to multimedia content directly to individual receiver and computer using a small satellite antenna without requiring any telephone or Internet connectivity.

- **Streaming Audio:** Internet, popularly called web, is a huge network of computers spread over the globe. The computers dedicated to provide information for other computers are called 'servers' and the computers that receive information from these servers are known as 'clients'. You can access Internet by connecting your computer through a telephone line or other communication network to the server of an Internet service provider. You can connect to any server on the Internet by logging on (connecting) it through it's unique address e.g. www.ignou.ac.in - the address of IGNOU's web site (server). When you are connected to a server, the information available on the server in the form of text, pictures, audio and video etc. is downloaded (brought) to your computer for display and listening, as per selections made by you. Due to technical limitations of the telephone line commonly used for Internet access, the download process may take appreciable time for downloading large sized information.

There are basically two ways to receive audio over the Web. The old way is by downloading audio files. In theory, audio files, like any other digital data, are suitable cargo for the Internet. But realistically, because high-quality audio files (e.g. WAV files) are huge in size, moving audio data across Internet takes enormous time. In normal transfer method, the user has to download a complete audio file to his computer and the file can be played only after the download is complete. Conventional downloading over telephone lines is a process that literally takes hours to yield a few minutes of sound.

The new way is by receiving "streamed" audio. Streaming is a technology for playing audio and video directly from a website. The old way involves long delays while the new way delivers instant sound. But like most emerging technologies, streamed audio is still experiencing growing pains.

Streamed audio technology is able to deliver real-time or "live" events over the Internet, called Web casting. Streaming audio being an Internet-based technology, can be accessed from anywhere in the world. Not surprisingly, more and more radio stations worldwide are getting interested in web casting the music, sports and news in a bid to broaden their reach. Streaming technology allows learners to access lengthy pre-recorded audio and video clips. Users can also watch or listen to a live event from a remote location. Streaming technology serves as a valuable means of delivering content for distributed learning programs. Streaming audio can provide a powerful medium for education. An instructor may offer all his lectures online. An online process is what is happening at that moment. These lectures can be stored for offline learning through "audio on demand". In this process the user is presented with an index of material stored on the server, from which s/he may choose a programme for listening. It shall provide an extra opportunity to the student who missed the lecture (online) and makes it possible for him to take notes and learn the material at the time of his choice. The streaming audio has several possibilities including the following:

- On-line lectures, recorded interviews, etc.
- Music teaching, for instance, a streaming audio file would be valuable to a music teacher. While going through the textual information, students shall also be able to listen to the related notes, music etc.

Chapter-5

Appropriate Technology

Q1. Define the basic concept of appropriate technology. Explain the criteria that decide appropriateness of technology for teaching-learning purpose.

Ans. The concept of appropriate technology is closely related to traditional technologies; it is designed for a particular community and it accounts for the environmental, cultural, social and economic aspects of that community. Appropriate technologies are "technologies with a human face", aimed at enabling people to earn a sustainable living. The concept of appropriate technology gained impetus with Schumacher's book Small is Beautiful (1973), where eight criteria were formulated for assessing technology"

(1) Appropriate technology best suits the needs and lifestyle of the people using it.

(2) Appropriate technology should not damage the environment and ecosystem and should be sustainable.

(3) Appropriate technology should keep costs within the economic means of a community.

(4) Appropriate technology should use locally available resources as far as possible.

(5) Appropriate technology should enable local workers to earn a living.

(6) Appropriate technology should increase self-reliance.

(7) Appropriate technology should use renewable sources of energy wherever possible and should be economical in its use of non-renewable resources.

(8) Appropriate technology should fit with its social and cultural environment.

The appropriateness of the technology depends on the context/situation in which it is to be used. When we intend to use technology in the field of education, we have to bear in mind that it is one of the means for making learning effective. In no way should it be allowed to become an end in itself. Using technology for its own sake overruling all other considerations amounts to technology dominating the teaching-learning scenario. So the goal should not be of 'using technology', but 'making use of technology' to reach the goals. More specifically speaking, the objectives of an educational programme are to be achieved through the aid of appropriately chosen technology.

To make our educational system technological, for the purpose of teaching and learning is being widely advocated at all levels of education and already a large number of educational institutions is gearing up for it. However, we have to keep in mind that before taking the plunge and opting for a particular technology it has to be thoroughly evaluated for its effectiveness in facilitating learning. It has to be adjudged, which particular technology would be appropriate for integration into the teaching-learning process.

This is because all these adjectives are contextual to the teaching-learning situation. As has been rightly mentioned by Kumar (1996), educational technology includes in the ambit 'systematic way of applying techniques' to achieve certain objectives and it is as important as the technology itself. Hence technology has to be chosen and applied in such a way that instruction can be imparted with a scientific base and is made more powerful.

There are following criteria's which should be kept in mind while deciding the appropriateness of technology for teaching learning purpose:

(1) Learner: A technology could be appropriate only if it suits the requirements of the learners. For learners with difficulty in reading, print medium whether on paper or as text in computer will not be appropriate and audio could be appropriate. For young children with less attention span lengthy radio talks, recorded discussions would not be appropriate. Powerful visuals would be required to retain their attention. Technology that allows greater control by learners through play back systems, facility for browsing is more suitable from the learners' point of view. Broadcasts and telecast do not allow learning at one's own pace. Their fixed timings also curtail the freedom and flexibility of their use and hence may not be fully appropriate when viewed from this angle. Size of the learners group is also important. Projected media, audio-visual media can be appropriate for large groups. The ability of the learner to operate the technological devices like computer also determines the appropriateness of technology.

(2) Teacher: Pedagogical value of technology also depends on the ability and the will of the teacher to extract full benefit out of it. A technology with all its pedagogical strengths may be inappropriate if the teacher cannot operate it. For instance, not all teachers can handle a projector and the films may get damaged. Preparing slides also requires certain skills. Even the tape of a simple audio cassette may get entangled if it is not placed properly. Many teachers are yet to develop the competence to use computers. Again some do not have a positive attitude towards technology for teaching.

(3) Content: The nature of the content to be taught is to be considered for judging which technology would be appropriate. For content related to historical process or architecture, video programmes, films and slides could be appropriate. For content related to numerical data, print teletext through computers could be a better choice (Bates, 1984). When the content is such that the learning has to proceed through logically arranged arguments and counter arguments then discussions, debates recorded in audio programmes would be appropriate. But when, content involves comparisons, say of healthy tissues and diseased ones, multi image technique involving simultaneous projections of more than one visual through slides/transparencies, video would be more appropriate.

(4) Method of Teaching: Today education are in favour of constructivism whereby the learner explores, discovers and constructs knowledge and thereby develops mental abilities such as reasoning, analysing, inferring, etc. Hence technology that allows self learning through exploring, discovering and processing the information obtained through computer and the Internet are suitable.

(5) Affordability: A particular technology can be deemed to be appropriate only if it does not strain the financial resources. The technology selected has to be cost effective, i.e. for the input in terms of cost, the output i.e., benefits accrued from the technology should be to the maximum extent. The cost factor is therefore to be considered for the evaluation of the appropriateness of technology. While selecting technology it has to be seen that the escalation in costs is not unrealistic.

The cost factor associated with technology is of special significance in the developing nations. Budgetary allocations of schools often may not permit the use of sophisticated technology. Hence inexpensive ones like certain audio-visual devices could be appropriate in situations with lower budgets. Such technology can be procured at a low price and also do not require costly infrastructure. Expensive technical devices like projector, computers, etc. lying unused in schools are not uncommon. This makes investment in such technology wasteful. Lack of funds to set up infrastructure necessary to operate them or the lack of competence &/ attitude of the teachers may be the factors that have come in the way of their use.

(6) Ease of Use: One of the criteria for adjudging a technology as modern is its being 'user friendly' i.e. the user should find it easy to operate and use. For example the cumbersome cameras of the past that had to be covered with a black cloth for photography have been replaced by digital cameras and automatic ones that can click photographs themselves and even help develop prints within no time. Similarly speedy and portable printers are replacing the heavier ones. Soft wares for computers are now-a-days developed in such a way that even a novice can use them. Since the last several years windows with icons have done away with the need to memorise the keys or their combinations for different functions.

(7) Maintainability: Maintenance of technology ensures that they prove to be cost effective in the long run i.e., from the investment made in technology; benefits can be accrued for a long time if there is proper maintenance. Maintaining technological devices requires expertise and skill. In case of certain technical devices the user may enter into a special contract with the vendor who takes up the responsibility of regular maintenance. Printed text, radio, television, slides, transparencies, etc. need minimum maintenance. Audio and video tapes also may get damaged but CD and DVD are more durable. But infrastructure for Internet and conferencing facilities need care.

Q2. What are the strengths and weaknesses of different types of technology?

Ans.

Table : Strengths and Weaknesses of Different Types of Technology

Technology	Strength	Weakness
Print technology	Portable, economic, easy to produce update and store, independent of infrastructure requirements, easily maintained conveys voluminous information, and allows easy browsing	Impact on learner lesser since only one sense (sight) is used.
Projected media slides, transparencies, still pictures, film strips) Audio technology	Helps in visual identification can show enlarged versions easy to produce, economic, p0rtable, can teach groups Radio reaches vast millions, useful for rapid dissemination of information, economic, portable, stimulates imagination, easily accessible; Cassettes & CDs allow learners greater control.	Audio effect is lacking. Films are fragile than slides, does not allow browsing Lacking in visuals, unsuitable for certain types of learning such as processes
Audio Visual Technology	Can capture live events, helps in retention of learning since two senses are involved, cassettes and CD-ROM allow replay, DVDs and videotapes can smoothly join frames and present continuous flow of visuals or enhance time intervals, easy to duplicate	Expensive, not so portable, infrastructure requirements are there; production cost is high, difficult to upgrade
Satellite-mediated communication technology	Audio and video conferencing provide interactivity with immediate feedback; Can connect and reach highly scattered learners	Expensive, heavy capital investments required
Computer	Multidimensional effect, provide text, visuals and sound, can provide simulation effects, storing, processing & retrieval of information easy	Desktops unlike laptops and simputers not portable; expensive
CDROM	May include content in multimedia format with hyperlinking & navigation facilities	A computer is needed to run it. Learner can control pace of

		learning.
Internet	Vast repertoire of information that can be surfed and downloaded, global knowledge and local resources like libraries (through local area networks) can be accessed, Aids constructivist learning. Allows usage of other techniques like chat, e mail. Conferencing, exchange of Ipods, long distance telephonic calls economically etc.	Expensive and needs complicated infrastructure
Conferencing facilities (audio, audio-video, computer)	Helps online seminars, group discussions, meetings, etc.	Expensive and needs complicated infrastructure

Q3. What do you mean by technology obsolescence? Write the ways to counter technology obsolescence.

Or

What is technology obsolescence? Explain any two methods to counter this.

Ans. Technology Obsolescence refers to the stage when an existing technology and its related products, services or processes may be replaced due to arrival of new technologies/innovations in the markets— thus making existing technology and its related products, services or processes degraded/obsolete.

At this stage, many applications of the existing technology lose relevance in the markets due to arrival of some alternative new technology. There are minimal sales of products/services based on remaining surviving few applications considered somewhat useful by the markets/consumers.

This stage is also sometimes called as Technology Decline Degraded Technology and calls for faster movement to newer technological opportunities. Technology obsolescence may occur due to some of following reasons:

- Increase in stock of technological knowledge in a nation
- Time-bound schedule for withdrawal of certain technologies might have been prescribed by the government authorities either as part of national technology strategy, or in the case of

hazardous, unsafe, unhealthy, polluting, outdated, primary technologies viz. withdrawal of older and polluting automobile technologies in India

- Development and arrival of new, better and improved technologies and innovations in the marketplace.
- Opening up and integration of national economy with international economy thus making some of the current national technologies obsolete due to presence of more advanced technologies at international level.
- It may be part of corporate technology strategy to gradually phase out older current technology and replace it with newer technologies so as to maintain technology leadership in the marketplace.
- High costs associated with using existing technologies like high manufacturing costs, higher wastages, high costs of waste disposal, higher costs of environment management.
- Encouragement and fiscal incentives may be given by the central government to move from fossil fuel based technologies to environment friendly and renewable energy technologies
- Actions and resistance by trade unions, consumer associations and non-government organisations may force the corporate managements to move towards environment friendly technologies and safer technologies
- Fast change in customer needs, tastes and preferences may make existing technologies obsolete.

Obsolescence of technology can be dealt with in the following ways:

- Upgrading technical abilities of a device by adding to it new facilities and making it more powerful can be done. For example a computer may later be fitted with a CD drive. It is however, advisable to go for up-gradation of an obsolete technology only to the extent to which it can take it. For instance to have sophisticated features like the Internet, pen drive, etc. it is better not to invest in a very old computer.
- To keep away the problem of obsolescence for a longer time it is advisable to invest in the latest one available.

- If it is affordable to discard old technology in favour of new ones then, anticipating the impending obsolescence, it may be done prior to the technological getting totally obsolete. It would make reselling difficult and these issues have to be considered at the planning and budgeting stage (Kistan, 1996).
- Continuing with obsolete technology till they function reasonably well. This would be economic and also save the institution from the necessity of training its staff to use new ones. This practice of 'amortising' otherwise obsolete technology could work especially well if there is proper maintenance and care. Depreciation of computer being rapid, amortisation i.e., deliberate decision to continue with obsolete technology is done more commonly.

Q4. Describe two technologies in the field of education that are on the verge of becoming obsolete today.

Ans. Technologies which are on the verge of becoming obsolete today are as follows:

(1) TVs and radios that need tuning: People on television and radio still occasionally say "stay tuned" when they are really asking you not to switch off or change the channel. The phrase lost its original meaning and your children will never guess that you used to turn a tiny dial like a safe cracker in an effort to get your TV tuned to the correct channel. Not content with the fiddliness of this process, some television manufacturers supplied their sets with a tiny plastic stick that had to be inserted into the tuner so you could find your channel. If you lost your tiny stick, the entire set was rendered useless.

(2) Video and audio tape: Tape is already a thing of the past in most homes. There's no need to remember to rewind a rental video before you return it and no need to spool back and forth to hear your favourite song on an album. The language remains, however, and your children may wonder why you talk about "taping" a TV show when what you're actually doing is saving it to a hard drive on a 'personal video recorder' (PVR). Your PVR lists each programme you've saved and even lets you start watching at a specific point. If you explain to your children that you used to have to fast-forward through your video cassette to see whether you taped Only Fools and Horses before or after last week's Question Time, they'll think you're having them on.

Q5. What is media mix? How it can be optimize?

Ans. Media mix can be defined as the combination of different media for the purpose of educational teaching-learning.

Printed materials, radio counseling, TV programmes, etc. may be offered to the learners for a particular course. Whatever media mix is made available to a student or groups of students for a given learning task, effort should be made to ensure that it is put to optimal usage. Planning the media mix judiciously is important and care has to be taken that the pedagogic weakness of one medium is supplemented by the strength of another included in the mix. For instance, videos may be prepared to depict processes that has been discussed in the print.

A reliable and if necessary a speedy feedback mechanism should be in operation so as to learn where the media mix might be failing or may be succeeded. For instance, why learners use only the print medium and ignore the other media could be found out through studies. Sometimes it may not be possible to replace the failed component of the media mix but the information obtained via feedback/research may help make a subsequent change. Many a times such information is only reflected in the examination results, making it imperative to monitor the performances, especially when the success or failure is visible in large number of cases, and reach conclusions about how the shortcoming may be overcome to optimise the media mix. For instance, if the learners fail to depict a process demonstrated in videos, then either the learners did not care to watch it or the video was ineffective. Then the video component of the media mix would need to be considered.

Designing a media mix involves:

- relating learning objectives and content to the media available;
- originating the design because no scientific formula for a particular design;
- assigning varying quantities of media to different courses, an ability most institutions find always limited; and
- moving rapidly from one medium to another, an ability most learners find imposes limitations.

After designing a media mix, institutions decide on the 'main medium' of communication and then decide how they can best use 'supporting' media.

In more formal systems:

- the main medium tends to be print; and
- face-to-face and electronic media take a supporting role.

In less formal systems:

- the broadcast of recorded media tends to take the lead;
- face-to-face contact provides focus; and
- print is used as additional support.

Mixed mode institution offers learners:

- a wide choice of modes of study independent, group-based, or some combination;
- and face-to-face, mediated, or some combination;
- maximises flexibility of place and pace of study;
- the result of 'convergence' of face-to-face and distance modes; and
- increasingly characterises organisations that were once 'single mode' or 'dual mode'.

Q6. Explain the concept of technology integration in teaching-learning process.

Ans. Technology Integration can be defined as the use of technology tools in education in order to allow students to apply computer and technology skills to learning and problem-solving. The tools of technology integration are computers, mobile devices like smart phones and tablets, digital cameras, social media platforms and networks, software applications, the Internet, etc. -- in daily classroom practices, and in the management of a school. Successful technology integration is achieved when the use of technology is:

- Routine and transparent,
- Accessible and readily available for the task at hand,
- Supporting the curricular goals, and helping the students to effectively reach their goals.

When technology integration is at its best, a child or a teacher doesn't stop to think that he or she is using a technology tool -- it is second nature. And students are often more actively engaged in projects when technology tools are a seamless part of the learning process.

Willingness to embrace change is also a major requirement for successful technology integration. Technology is continuously, and rapidly, evolving. It is an ongoing process and demands continual learning.

When effectively integrated into the curriculum, technology tools can extend learning in powerful ways. These tools can provide students and teachers with:

- Access to up-to-date, primary source material.
- Methods of collecting/recording data.
- Ways to collaborate with students, teachers, and experts around the world.
- Opportunities for expressing understanding via multimedia.
- Learning that is relevant and assessment that is authentic.
- Training for publishing and presenting their new knowledge.

Types of Technology Integration: It is sometimes difficult to describe how technology can impact learning because the term "technology integration" is such a broad umbrella that covers so many varied tools and practices; there are many ways technology can become an integral part of the learning process. These ways are listed below but new technology tools and ideas emerge daily:

- **Online Learning and Blended Classrooms:** While K-12 online learning gains traction around the world, many teachers are also exploring blended learning -- a combination of both online and face-to-face education.
- **Project-Based Activities Incorporating Technology:** Many of the most rigorous projects are infused with technology from start to finish. Schools are getting excellent results from mixing PBL with a one-to-one laptop program.
- **Game-Based Learning and Assessment:** There has been a lot of buzz about the benefits of incorporating simulations and game-based learning activities into classroom instruction.
- **Learning with Mobile and Handheld Devices:** Once widely dismissed as distractions, devices like cell phones, mp3 players, and tablet computers are now being used as learning tools in forward-thinking schools.
- **Instructional Tools like Interactive Whiteboards and Student Response Systems:** In many schools, the days of green chalkboards are over.

- **Web-Based Projects, Explorations, and Research:** One of the first, and most basic, ways that teachers encouraged kids to use technology is with online research, virtual field trips, and webquests.
- **Student-Created Media like Podcasts, Videos, or Slideshows:** One of the central ideas of digital or media literacy is that students should be come creators and critics, not just consumers, of media.
- **Collaborative Online Tools like Wikis or Google Docs:** Connecting with others online can be a powerful experience, both for teachers and for students.
- **Using Social Media to Engage Students:** Though social media tools are still blocked in many schools, students around the world spend vast amounts of time on social networks outside of school.

Q7. What are the guidelines for teachers for the integration of technology in education?

Ans. The major guidelines for integration of technology have been discussed below:

(1) The teacher has to ensure that when the learners get an access to a vast amount of information and facts, they do not stray from their focus. The pedagogical approach to integrate technology as required by Rogers (2000) is that the teacher should select the content and accordingly choose the tools. This would require them to explore the technological resources available. He/she should frame the objectives of learning and clearly interpret the guidelines regarding the tasks and sub tasks to be performed by the learners. Monitoring learning and evaluation of learning outcomes remain as important as ever. The learners can also subject themselves to self-evaluation through tests and/or quizzes with the help of computers, while accessing instructions through it.

(2) The teachers have to be reflective and evolve suitable instructional strategies to integrate technology. Also, they have to adapt to a new role-facilitator of learning from being the sole source of information. Then only integration would be possible.

(3) Teachers should design developmentally appropriate learning strategies to support unique needs of the learner. The teacher has to consider the learner's readiness for learning and that to with technology,

previous knowledge, the technology to be selected activities to be taken up by them and other such details and chalk out appropriate instructional strategies.

(4) Teacher becomes a facilitator and manager of learning rather than some one who provides learners with every information.

(5) Teachers should use technology to foster higher order cognitive abilities in learners. In Bloom's Taxonomy of learning, knowledge (memory level) is at lowest level of cognition. It is preceded by comprehension, application, analysis and synthesis. The learner even if provided with the best technological resources like the Internet may confine himself only to the task of collecting information or facts. He/she has to be provided with suitable cognitive challenges so as to foster the higher cognitive abilities. If learners process information through acts of comparing, contrasting, analysing, synthesising and drawing inferences, their critical thinking and problem solving abilities will be fostered.

Q8. Discuss the criteria for the assessment of integration of technology in education.

Ans. For assessing the integration of technology in the teaching-learning process we need to consider following criteria:

Assessment of Integration of Technology: While we try to assess the integration of technology in the teaching learning process, we may consider these criteria:

(1) The expertise of the teacher in operating the technology is important but more important is to harness it as a tool for teaching.

(2) There has to be appropriateness for:

- Information, i.e. richness, adequacy, relevance and accuracy of the content.
- Instruction-How far the software can support learning.
- Instructional designing- at which point, which technology is used and for what purpose and the designing of the software delivered

(3) How well technology has been infused in the activities of the classroom, from teaching to administration.

(4) In case of distance learning and also in face to face situations, how judiciously technology has been selected and at what points of the content they are being integrated.

(5) The software is also important and rather than its being more of a source of information, it has to be a tool for providing instructions.

Ultimately the aim is to assess how well the objectives of the course have fulfilled. This should be the guiding factor for any assessment rather than the variety and how advanced the technologies integrated are. With regards of above mentioned points along with them we need to assess the level of integration of technology as follows:

(1) Integration of technology: The teacher and learner both use technology for teaching and learning purposes respectively. Technology is also used for administrations and activities supplementing teaching.

(2) Adoption of technology: The teacher begins to use technology for delivering instructions

(3) Exploration: The teacher determines why and which technology is needed. S/he then collects information about the technological resources and knows how to use them.

Q9. Write a short note on Dexter's e-tips or principles about integrating technology.

Ans. Dexter (2002) has formulated certain 'e tips' or principles that would help in integrating technology. These tips are premised on two dimensions – the classroom, which is managed by the teacher and the school that comes under the school administrators. These e-tips can be discussed as follows:

(1) Classroom Level e-tips:

(i) Technology on its own is devoid of any inherent instructional value. Hence, the teacher must consider what added value can be obtained through it and utilise technological resources wisely to facilitate learning.

(ii) The teacher should use technology for assessment of learning outcomes. Computerised quizzes, recorded oral questionnaires on an audio cassette player, etc. can help in the process of assessment.

(iii) The teacher must devote time and attention to devise appropriate teaching strategies. Only with an appropriate strategy can the full potential of technology be harnessed. A strategy comprising objectives of learning, the tasks necessary to achieve them the type and combination to technological devices to be used, the stage of teaching-learning at which they are to be used, etc. is to be formulated.

(2) School Level e-tip;

(i) It is the duty of teacher education institutes to ensure that teachers are capable of integrating technology. Their efforts often fall far short in this respect. Training should be provided to equip the teachers with the know how to successfully integrate technology.

(ii) For integration of technology the first and foremost requirement is that teacher and learners should have an access to technological devices. It is the duty of the school to provide them.

Q10. Describe the barriers to the process of technology integration.

Ans. The elimination of hte barriers prevailing is important for successful integration process. There are following major barriers to technology integration:

(1) Availability of the necessary infrastructure: This is indispensable for technology integration. For instance, having a television or computers is not enough. There must be electricity to operate them. Again, when computers are not there in sufficient number, computer based teaching and learning and web based instructions would not be possible. Also, if the desired bandwidth is unavailable working on the Internet would be a slow process.

(2) **Government Policies:** Unless policies are there to integrate technology in education, the process may not be accorded the importance it deserves. Policies at the state level may require the educational institutions to integrate technology. As for instance, in many institutions there are directives for teachers to do so because of the encouraging policies framed and implemented. There is also a need for financial support for investing in technologies and there should be policies to this effect.

(3) Curriculum: The curriculum should be flexible and learner centred to include activities that require the use of technology for learning. Rather than a curriculum that emphasises bookish knowledge and rote learning, one which has the flexibility to provide ample scope for constructive learning through assignments and projects will encourage integration of technology.

(4) Inadequate access to technology: Access to not only advanced technologies but also the relatively simple ones is difficult. There are many schools where even charts and slides are unavailable. As discussed earlier, in the case of distant learning before integration of technology the access to it of the target group has to be considered.

(5) Evaluation pattern: In an educational system, dominated by evaluation and in which product evaluation rather than process evaluation is important, there is lesser scope for technology integration. Teachers and learners remain busy with ways traditional ways of learning that would ensure better grades at the term end examinations than on activities that integrate technology.

(6) Overcrowded classrooms: High teacher – student ratio are not conducive for integration of technology within the classroom.

(7) Training teachers: Teachers need to be trained to enable them to use technology.

(8) Lack of positive attitude on the part of the teacher: Compared to medicine, defence, agriculture and many other fields, technology integration in the field of education has been quite slow and to a lesser degree. Still the traditional method of lecturing is followed. This is partly because of the apathy of the teachers and a negative attitude towards technology. There is still a hesitation to handle technological devices.

(9) Lack of support of administrators: School level e-tips, discussed earlier underline that for technology integration teachers need the support of the school administration, Procuring technology, setting up the infrastructure for it, training teachers, etc. are the factors that have to be managed by the administration.

Q11. Explain the importance of convergence and miniaturisation of technology.

Ans. Information and communication technology helped in the profound transformation of educational teaching-learning. The process of advancement in education tells the importance of convergence and miniaturisation of technology. This process can be discussed as follows:

Convergence of technology: In the past technological devices used only one medium. For instance a radio or an audio tape recorder were audio aids. They did not have the capacity to show the visuals. The films and televisions were the beginning points of integration of media. The computers take us a step further. Apart from audio and video facilities it can also give us access to texts. Convergence of technologies underlies the modern trend in education. It leads to the merging of digital communication technologies, computing and digital media and the resulting technology can facilitate communication, computing, education, entertainment, etc. round the clock through a single device, which can be as small as a cell phone. This facility through telecom and IT networks. Is facilitating teaching and learning and making it a collaborative processes.

Convergence of technologies for computing and telecommunications enables access to information in multimedia through a single device. Hence, there is the demand for a system that allows the merger of technologies. Technologies that otherwise operate separately and singularly are now synergistically combined for heightening the efficiencies of the resulting converged technology.

Converged technologies make learning interactive and can enrich it by linking users to sources of information as the Internet or even online libraries. It thus converts the learning scenario into a virtual classroom. An example of converged technology is the cell phone, increasingly incorporating different technologies such as the digital cameras, mp3 player (digital audio player), camcorder (digital camera with facility for capturing both video as well as audio), voice recorder, etc. They can also be used as computing devices and also connect the user to the Internet.

Convergence combines three major technologies - broadcasting, telecommunication and computing and information is shared as content that can be processed, stored and exchanged as per the convenience of the users and this has immense potential for distance education. Today technology integration may require a multimedia arrangement with teachers and learners resorting to several different devices like radio, TV, computer, phone, etc. But convergence of technology will enable learners to get all the facilities through a single device. Hence, cell phone may be that device in the coming days.

Miniaturisation of technology: Miniaturisation can be defined as "to make a version of something in a much smaller size or on a greatly reduced scale". In technology applications, the word miniaturization deals with the basic dimensions of the actual technology itself. In other words, miniaturization is making our electronic devices that we use everyday smaller and smaller. Wikipedia gives a better definition by stating that miniaturization is the progression of mechanical, optical, and electronic devices to decrease in size.

The process of miniaturization and the generation of miniatures, which are integral facets of the digital, yield affective responses as it is the phase miniaturisation of everything. As users encounter virtual miniaturization and miniatures, they experience sensations of intimacy, possession or control with respect to the digital data obtained through networked computer screens. These effects are characteristic of the way that the human body determines to a large extent what constitutes a technique of miniaturization and the dimension of a miniature. The sensations of intimacy, possession or control are also evoked by both the practice of miniaturization and the fashioning of miniatures that mark the rise of the printing press, photography and television. Although new media provide distinct forms of miniaturization and miniatures, this progression toward diminution is rooted in earlier technologies.

Example: Mr. X, a student of Management Studies, carries a laptop to his college to acquire, feed and store information. Mrs. Y, a wildlife photographer does her job with a handy cam. Mr. A carries a ring-size video camera for observing children at play.

Such miniaturised technology has now reached the field of education. Small sized radio, hand held video cameras or handy cams (camcorders), laptops, portable computers and notebooks and even palmtops i.e. hand held computers are common today. Today there are also hand held personal digital assistants. Miniaturisation of technology has been aided by wire free systems. Transistors, cell phones, computers, etc. can be operated without wired connections. Portable and small sized hard drives with huge data storing capacity are available.

Miniaturisation of technology not only makes the tools light and handy and hence portable but also helps in individualising education. Every individual learner who has an access to a laptop shall learn at his/her own pace and in his/her own style. We can visualise a scene when the school bag shall have a computer instead of books and notebooks.

Q12. Discuss the concept of technology as a surrogate teacher.

Or

Discuss strengths and limitations of technology as a surrogate teacher.

Ans. Text is one of the earliest of learning aids while information and communication technology (ICT) is obviously much more recent. The support for understanding which text might supply through a surrogate teacher (text as tutor) analogy. This analogy is also applied to ICT but, as ICT may function in a variety of ways, it needs to be seen from other viewpoints. These include the computer as a tool, as a simulator of the world, and as a provider of learning environments. Different people may not learn equally well from different teaching and learning aids so this needs to be taken into account.

A surrogate teacher is something which has the role of a teacher. For instance, when instructional radio was introduced in 1932 in the USA, it was described as the Assistant Teacher. Television had a similar role when Samoa was faced with a teacher shortage. In the 1960s, between a quarter and a third of the Samoan school day was spent watching televised lessons and the remaining time was given to activities based on them. Australia and New Zealand have supported education in remote communities in similar ways. Distance learning systems tend to be, in effect, teachers for those who must learn at home. These systems can include a wide range of learning aids such as video recordings, computer-based instruction and textual materials to provide a guided didactic conversation.

Advantages

(1) Higher cognitive processes are encouraged when information is processed through analysis, synthesis, etc. It encourages critical thinking and problem solving abilities.

(2) Education is individualised as every learner learns at his/her own pace and in his/her own style. It thus addresses various styles and paces of learning.

(3) The learners learn to explore and discover sources of information. Accessing a global pool of knowledge imparts a global outlook to the students.

(4) Technology provides access to a vast source of the latest knowledge and information from all over the world that can be stored, retrieved, updated and reused.

(5) Human beings cannot cope up with the knowledge explosion. Hence teachers cannot always provide authentic and current

information. Technology helps us in getting authentic and current information.

(6) Technology carries learning material to individuals irrespective of their geographical location. It thus makes the society egalitarian and democratises education.

(7) It engage learners through out the learning process and motivates through assessment of learning progress and feedback. It also allows interactions. Instructions through many technologies can be used and reused and stopped and started at will. Thus learning is learner centered.

Limitation

(1) Long exposure to TV and computer screens from childhood affects health. Continued exposure to the glare of the computer screen may affect the eyesight Sedentary habits rob individuals of physical exercise.

(2) It may make learners, especially children averse to socialising in a face to face manner.

(3) Technology can never substitute the humane elements of a teacher like the ability to inspire and guide with a human touch, provide warmth, affection and leadership, and inculcate values.

(4) Access to too much information can confuse a young learner and lead him/her astray from the focus.

(5) Modern schools in a bid to offer progressive education, allot more time for computers and Internet. It is taking a toll on lessons in art, music and games. Aesthetic, social and physical developments may thus get neglected.

(6) Internet/TV have hypnotic effects that can hook people and make them addicted to it.

(7) Integration of technology requires great capital investment. Apart from physical resources, recruiting trained manpower to operate them also requires financial inputs.

Q13. What do you mean by professional development? Discuss professional development in the context of technical educational training.

Ans. In education, the term professional development can be used in reference to a wide variety of specialized training, formal education, or advanced professional learning intended to help administrators, teachers, and other educators improve their professional knowledge, competence, skill, and effectiveness.

In practice, professional development for educators encompasses an extremely broad range of topics and formats. For example, professional development experiences may be funded by district, school, or state budgets and programs, or they may be supported by a foundation grant or other private funding source. They may range from a one-day conference to a two-week workshop to a multiyear advanced-degree program. They may be delivered in person or online, during the school day or outside of normal school hours, and through one-on-one interactions or in group situations. And they may be led and facilitated by educators within a school or provided by outside consultants or organizations hired by a school or district. And, of course, the list of possible formats could go on.

The following are a representative selection of common professional development topics and objectives for educators:

- Furthering education and knowledge in a teacher's subject area—e.g., learning new scientific theories, expanding knowledge of different historical periods, or learning how to teach subject-area content and concepts more effectively.
- Training or mentoring in specialized teaching techniques that can be used in many different subject areas, such as differentiation (varying teaching techniques based on student learning needs and interests) or literacy strategies (techniques for improving reading and writing skills), for example.
- Earning certification in a particular educational approach or program, usually from a university or other credentialing organization, such as teaching Advanced Placement courses or career and technical programs that culminate in students earning an industry-specific certification.
- Developing technical, quantitative, and analytical skills that can be used to analyze student-performance data, and then use the findings to make modifications to academic programs and teaching techniques.
- Learning new technological skills, such as how to use interactive whiteboards or course-management systems in

ways that can improve teaching effectiveness and student performance.

- Improving fundamental teaching techniques, such as how to manage a classroom effectively or frame questions in ways that elicit deeper thinking and more substantive answers from students.
- Working with colleagues, such as in professional learning communities, to develop teaching skills collaboratively or create new interdisciplinary courses that are taught by teams of two or more teachers.
- Developing specialized skills to better teach and support certain populations of students, such as students with learning disabilities or students who are not proficient in English.
- Acquiring leadership skills, such as skills that can be used to develop and coordinate a school-improvement initiative or a community-volunteer program.
- Pairing new and beginning teachers with more experienced "mentor teachers" or "instructional coaches" who model effective teaching strategies, expose less-experienced teachers to new ideas and skills, and provide constructive feedback and professional guidance.
- Conducting **action research** to gain a better understanding of what's working or not working in a school's academic program, and then using the findings to improve educational quality and results.
- Earning additional formal certifications, such as the National Board for Professional Teaching Standards certification, which requires educators to spend a considerable amount of time recording, analyzing, and reflecting on their teaching practice (many states provide incentives for teachers to obtain National Board Certification).
- Attending graduate school to earn an advanced degree, such as a master's degree or doctorate in education, educational leadership, or a specialized field of education such as literacy or technology.

Q14. Discuss the types of simulation in the context of technology in education.

Ans. Simulation can be used for explaining theoretical concepts to allowing learners to take managerial decisions in an artificial environment. Simulations have models of real/imagined situations that are in reality inaccessible due to costs, logistics, dangers, etc. Students interact with such learning situations to learn. Dissections of animals in artificial laboratories, financial transactions at stock exchanges, driving automobiles, flying aircrafts, etc. can be learnt in simulated situations.

There are following types of simulation for technology in education:

(1) Equipment simulation: This is perhaps the most common usage of simulation technology. The creation of a simulated environment to teach the intricacies involved in a machine is a very effective way of teaching. Equipment simulation goes beyond machine and can help in creating a factory environment too which can help in studying various design options and logistics involved in such design. Similarly a simulated laboratory may be created.

(2) The management simulation: This enables learners to exercise their options for managerial decisions. Modere (Motivation, Desire, Result) is a knowledge-based simulation, which provides a human resource manager various combinations of motivational factors and their impact on the efficiency of the workers. Modere is an interesting simulation to look into human resource problems. It helps the learner (a human resource person in this case) learn the skills of human resource (HR) management, motivation and rewards for personnel. The HR manager enters information about the person, the reward policy of the company, action proposed by the person and a description of the social environment. The manager then runs the simulation and observes the consequences on the levels of satisfaction action and frustration of the candidate and how these evolve in time. By changing parameters, like the date of the salary rise or a new job appointment, the HR manager can make adjustments to find the best solution.

(3) Distributed Interactive Simulation (DIS): This technology was developed by the US Advanced Research Project. It enables networking of hundreds of low-cost person-in-the-loop tank and aircraft simulators and imparts improved tactical team training. The soldiers practice their professional skills in synthetic battlefield. There are several simulations which are geographically distributed and these simulations are then made to interact in a common virtual environment.

Ravet & Layte, 1997 explained following things which DIS makes possible:

(i) assessment of group performance;

(ii) evaluation of new tactics;

(iii) testing new weapon systems;

(iv) practice of the combined arms tactics;

(v) assessment of equipment operator's performance.

The key issue in learning through simulation is not that of how well the simulation performed but that of how much of the learned skills are taken back by the learners to their real world of work. After successfully completing the training with simulations the success attained should get translated in achieving the required level of performance in real situations.

Simulations have also been developed in the field of engineering, electric/and electronics, etc. By providing a learner an independent electronic circuit, the simulation allows the learner to explore the existing circuit, modify it and observe the results gradually leading to making a new circuit from scratch. Similarly; a better understanding of an existing design is facilitated with the help of simulation of such design.

(4) Theory simulation: Theory simulation explains the basic assumptions involved in a system and their impact on the end result. Mathematica is one example of theory simulation which has been developed by Wolfram Research, USA. It connects mathematics to real-life example. Students can manipulate the parameters of a document and can understand the impact of such manipulation on the document.

(5) Decision-Making: The process of decision-making is concurrent with the process of teaching and learning. The first big decision is regarding the selection of the best-suited technology to impart training (on the part of trainers/educators) and acceptance of such technology (on the part of learners). The fear of dealing with the technology selected or lack of minimum level of expertise needed to deal with such selected technology itself can pose a serious threat to whole idea of imparting new information.

Once the technology has been accepted then a series of activities like testing and validation of the technology and making decisions for the rest of the learning process are then undertaken. The kind of decisions made depend largely on the decision-making situations. The degree of decisions can vary from certainty to great uncertainty. The decision-making process can be divided into two main categories (Yahalom, 1995):

Descriptive: This relates to data collection and data processing.

Inferential: This relates to interpretation of information and decision-making.

For example, if a researcher conducts a survey about a product in terms of its demand by people and collects data, such data collection and further classification of such data on the basis of gender, age group, educational background and so forth is descriptive decision making process. If the above mentioned data collected through survey is put some statistical test to see if there is any correlation or other effect then it is known as inferential decision making. Here one does more analysis of data to arrive at a decision. This is one of the procedures adopted before an educational programme is launched.

Each profession has its specific needs, which a trainer/educator keeps in mind while imparting the new information. But broadly speaking, a learner can take judicious decision or find solutions to problems if he/she:

(i) Has comprehensive and specific knowledge of the field.

(ii) Receives proper guidance to use data and information.

(iii) Has framework of appropriate decisions to be taken in various situations.

(iv) Can think at a higher cognitive level.

(v) Has clear understanding of the basic assumptions involved.

All these tasks are facilitated by modern technologies like the computer that help in accessing data (over the Internet), processing it and utilising it for decision making. For instance, data of learners achievements over the years in a particular area can be stored, processed and utilised for decision making. There are softwares for collecting, disseminating, and dispatching information on a regular basis. Today, information on Internet-based services is continually updated and hence decision making is based on current data. Tools are also there that train in thinking and decision making in given situations. Such tools amy provide viable options and guiding principles for decision making. There are microworld simulations that help in training in dynamic decision making process in artificially created i.e. virtual complex environments.

(6) Modelling: Modelling has proved to be one of the most successful learning processes. In simulation the learner is given a model and s/he studies through it whereas in modelling, the learner is the creator of the model. It is very realistic to assume that with successive models a learner keeps improving his/her skill, which become useful in the real world situations like communication and testing skills.

There are five major phases of a modelling activity:

(i) Analyse the data.

(ii) Test the model by collecting data to validate the basic hypothesis underlying the model.

(iii) If the need by then change/modify the model.

(iv) One must describe the system/problem and its associated components.

(v) Define and structure the ideas within a model to communicate the relationship between the components.

For instance, a model of governance can be developed and tested for its effectiveness or a model to save energy in a university campus may be developed. It is possible that a particular system can be represented by different models. What makes the selection of one model over the other is the objective of the system and also the learning style of the individual. Another factor which contributes to making a particular model is the kind of modelling software package used. There could be an inherent tendency in a package, which favours particular type of modelling. There are many software packages available for modelling but for powerful packages one needs advanced progrmming skills to run them. And that is the reason for most of the learners to use spreadsheets since they are convenient to work with than programming languages.

Some models may be designed for routine in-service educational programmes as part of the endeavour towards professional development, while some models may be designed to fulfil a sudden emerging need i.e. that are just in time context. The learning through these programmes can be put to use immediately. Models of training may relate to previous experiences, have scope for self assessment, self correction, reflection, etc. i.e. it may includes features that promote metacognition.

Q15. Write a short on Telematics.

Ans. Telematics is the blending of computers and wireless telecommunications technologies, ostensibly with the goal of efficiently conveying information over vast networks to improve a host of business functions or government-related public services. The most notable example of telematics may be the Internet itself, since it depends on a number of computer networks connected globally through telecommunication backbones.

The term has evolved to refer to automobile systems that combine global positioning satellite (GPS) tracking and other wireless communications for automatic roadside assistance and remote diagnostics. General Motors Corp. first popularized automotive telematics with its OnStar system.

The telematics industry is not limited to automotive applications. Other applications are being studied or developed for monitoring water and air pollution, for medical informatics and health care, and for distance learning. Many countries are developing uniform policies to integrate telematics applications into government, business and education.

In distance learning learners can chat or send emails with files attached to exchange information with their peers and teachers and also other experts. Video and computer conferencing facilities are revolutioning seminars, conferences and meetings wherein the participants need not be physically present. Countries with highly developed infrastructure needed for Information and Communication Technology (ICT) and networks to support education and training are set to gain from the use of telematics for distance education and training.

Q16. Discuss the use of virtual reality. What are the types of virtual reality?

Ans. Virtual reality can create real world like environment through computers. Virtual education open a new world of experience and make the learning process a lot more real without learners actually having to go to the field. One such device is data-gloves which facilitates manoeuvring of three-dimensional objects on computer screen.

The term virtual reality was first used by Jaron Lanier in 1989. According to him a VR is a medium where a virtual world (a synthetic 3-D environment in colour and with stereo sound) can be explored and examined continuously from any perspective in real time. There is continuous control of one's movements and what is seen by one is in three-dimensional setting making it appear as a real world. A small movement triggers a change in the three-dimensional appearance of the image and enforces the experience of a real world change. VR has enables a new learning environment in terms of breadth and space. Now a learner is not an outsider in the events as they unfold in front of his/her eyes but very much in the middle of the events and also controls the events. He/she feels the sense of touching the real objects in a real world.

Types of Virtual Reality are as follows:

(1) Desktop VR: Desktop VR systems use a conventional computer monitor to display the virtual world. This would be akin to the now popular virtual environments such as Second Life, Open Simulator, or even some computer games. Conventional peripheral devices (e.g., computer mice or keyboards) are typically used to navigate these types of virtual worlds. Desktop VR lacks the full immersive capabilities of more advanced types of VR systems. However, desktop VR is still popular because it is relatively inexpensive compared to other types of VR systems.

(2) Projection VR: Projection VR involves the projection of an environment around the user so the user can interact with the projected environment directly. Simulation Virtual reality is defined as a situation where a virtual character within the simulation is given the identity of the user in the form of an "avatar". I n SVR the user can have the character do an activity, have facial expressions and interact with other avatars in the simulation. In desktop VR, a user views a three dimensional simulation of a procedure or an environment where a topic is illustrated via a computer monitor.

(3) Total immersion VR: Total immersion VR: It gives a feel a complete immersion in a different world by using special devices like helmets, gloves wearing specially designed suites. From educational point of view, this is of immense usage where one is learning while performing like practicing a surgery, playing a sport or acting in a play.

Q17. Discuss the main features of continuing professional development.

Or

Write the reasons behind adopting a technology for learning.

Or

Discuss the points which facilitate life-long learning.

Ans. Techniques of teaching are changing. It is becoming increasingly clear that initial training or qualifications will not be sufficient to meet an individual's or organisation's demands. The focus has shifted to the continual updating of skills and developing multiple skills to meet the ever changing socioeconomic demands. Need for life-long learning is being felt by professional as the intrinsic need of their professions.

The Main Features of Continuing Professional Development are as follows:

The key features of Continuing Professional Development (CPD) as given by *Ravet & Layte (1997) as follows:*

(1) Integration of learning and work: The concept of work as a learning experience.

(2) Emphasis on learning through an extremely wide range of activities.

(3) Ownership of CPD by the individual.

(4) Emphasis on outcomes: answering the questions 'What did you learn?' and 'How do you plan to apply this learning?' rather than simply 'What learning event did you experience?'

(5) Planned and systematic updating of professional knowledge and improvement of personal competence throughout the individual's working life.

Gradually the traditional way of imparting training through 'training course' is being replaced by a well-structured way of on-the-job learning. Any technology which is open and flexible to suit the convenience of the learner is of immense help in life-long learning.

Reason behind adopting any technology: The reasons behind adopting a technology, which enables an open and flexible learning environment are as follows:

(1) When more people enrol the relative cost of the training reduces substantially.

(2) It infuses a sense of responsibility amongst learners who set their own targets of learning and development.

(3) A person can decide about the place, time and pace of learning.

Gooley, Skippington & Towers (2001) provide a diagram, which highlights the points, which facilitate life-long learning in the context of rural and remote communities. The diagram is as follows:

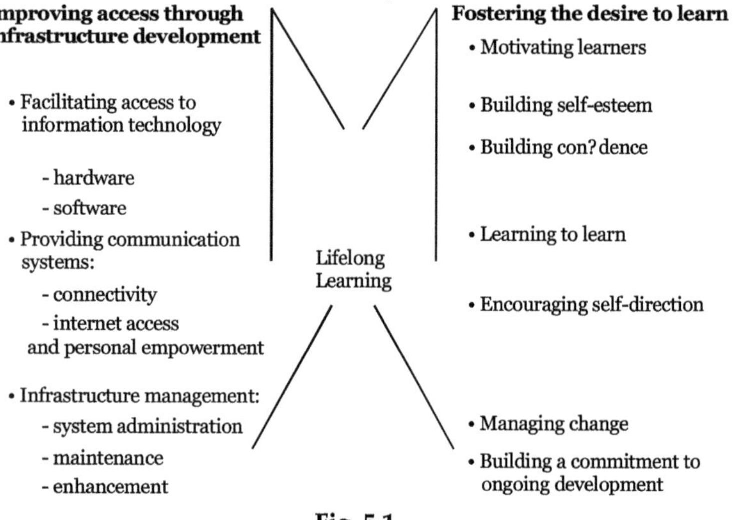

Fig. 5.1

❑❑❑

QUESTION PAPERS

Communication and Information Technology: MES-032

June, 2020

Note: All questions are compulsory. All questions carry equal weightage.

Q1. Answer the following question in about 600 words:

Define "Interactive Media". Explain the use of various interactive media for learning.

Or

Discuss general principles to be considered while planning communication for education and training. Support your answer with'an illustration.

Q2. Answer the following questions in about 600 words:

Discuss the types and use of various access devices for self-learning materials.

Or

Discuss the behaviourist theory of learning with its educational implications.

Q3. Answer any four of the following in about 150 words each:

(a) Telematics in training

(b) Technology as an aid for simulation

(c) Advantages and disadvantages of teleconferencing.

(d) Production Stages of an audio programme.

(e) Emerging trends in Broadcasting.

(f) Importance of interactivity in communication process.

Q4. Answer the following question in about 600 words:

Identify a topic of your choice and illustrate how you can integrate various technologies with teaching-learning process to teach that topic.

❑❑❑

Communication and Information Technology: MES-032

December, 2020

Note: (i) All questions are compulsory. (ii) All questions carry equal weightage.

Q1. Answer the following question in about 600 words:

What is meant by Self Instructional Material's (SLMs)? Discuss the important characteristics of SLMs.

Or

What is teleconferencing? Describe the threestep strategy to be adopted during a teleconferencing session to ensure good support between students and teacher.

Q2. Answer the following question in about 600 words:

Discuss different technologies used in classroom teaching.

Or

Explain barriers in communication. Suggest the strategies to overcome these barriers with suitable examples.

Q3. Answer any four of the following in about 150 words each:

(a) Potential of media mix in optimising the use of technology.

(b) Educational implications of 'stimulus response' theory of learning.

(c) Presentation formats of audio programmes.

(d) Advantages of computer conferencing technology.

(e) Computer graphics for material development.

(f) Differentiate between terrestrial and satellite based transmission of TV signals.

Q4. Answer the following question in about 600 words:

Identify a topic of your choice from secondary school curriculum and develop a plan to teach the same by integrating appropriate technology.

❑❑❑

Communication and Information Technology: MES-032

June, 2021

Note: All questions are compulsory. All questions carry equal weightage.

Q1. Answer the following question in about 600 words:

Compare operant conditioning with classical conditioning. Explain the educational implications of operant conditioning.

Or

Discuss the strengths and weaknesses of technology as a surrogate mother.

Q2. Answer the following question in about 600 words:

Explain the meaning of self-learning. Discuss the factors to be kept in mind while designing print materials for self-learning.

Or

Explain the concept of 'interactivity'. Discuss the use of various media which can improve interactivity in the teaching-learning process.

Q3. Write short notes on any four of the following in about 150 words each:

(a) Differences between formal and informal communication.

(b) Presentation formats of video programmes.

(c) Use of technology for professional development.

(d) Compare computer-based training with web-based training.

(e) Developmental testing to ensure quality of SLMs.

(f) Five steps of the SQ3R system for improving reading-skills.

Q4. Answer the following question in about 600 words:

Select a topic of your choice for producing a video programme and describe the steps you will follow from 'storyboard stage' to 'final programme production stage'.

❑❑❑

Communication and Information Technology: MES-032

December, 2021

Note: All questions are compulsory. All questions carry equal weightage.

Q1. Answer the following question in about 600 words:

Explain various types of teleconferencing. How does teleconferencing facilitate teaching and learning in distance education? Discuss with suitable examples.

Or

Discuss the importance of interactivity in the communication process. How can interactivity be enhanced in student learning? Explain with the help of suitable examples.

Q2. Answer the following question in about 600 words:

Discuss the significance of print medium in distance education system. Highlight various considerations to be kept in mind while developing print materials in distance education.

Or

Explain the meaning and use of Access Devices. Suggest various activities which can be designed as access devices to ensure active learning.

Q3. Write short notes on any four of the following in about 150 words each:

(a) Technology as a Surrogate Teacher.

(b) Various Presentation Formats of Video Programmes.

(c) Creating a Positive Learning Environment.

(d) Optimisation of Media Mix.

(e) Acoustic Design of a Studio.

(f) SQ3R System of Reading.

Q4. Answer the following question in about 600 words:

Select a topic of your choice on which you want to develop an audio programme. Choose the audio format and justify its choice. Which steps will you follow to produce the audio programme? Describe.

❑❑❑

Communication and Information Technology: MES-032

June, 2022

Note: (i) All questions are compulsory. (ii) All questions carry equal weightage.

Q1. Answer the following question in about 600 words:

Discuss the barriers to classroom communication. Suggest the measures to overcome these barriers.

Or

Describe the general principles of planning communication for education and training.

Q2. Answer the following question in about 600 words:

Explain various types of synchronous communication technologies. Discuss how the instruction is designed for teleconferencing.

Or

Discuss the factors appropriate for the use of technology in the teaching-learning process.

Q3. Answer any four of the following questions in about 150 words each:

(a) Differentiate between analog and digital audio format.

(b) Differentiate between computer and web-based training.

(c) Significance of print media in distance education.

(d) Devices for assistive technology for learning.

(e) Participatory approach to creating learning environment in classroom.

(f) Study skills to ensure effective learning.

Q4. Answer the following question in about 600 words:

Select a topic of your choice, suggest the technology integration plan you would adopt to optimise the learning experiences. Suggest the criteria you would use to assess the proposed integration of technology.

❑❑❑

www.ingramcontent.com/pod-product-compliance
Ingram Content Group UK Ltd.
Pitfield, Milton Keynes, MK11 3LW, UK
UKHW021703190726
13853UKWH00001B/406

9 789355 543936